LONGMAN LITERATURE

POEMS 2

Editors: Julia Markus and Paul Jordan

LONGMAN

New Longman Literature
Post-1914 Fiction

Susan Hill *I'm the King of the Castle* 0 582 22173 0
        The Woman in Black 0 582 02660 1
        The Mist in the Mirror 0 582 25399 3
Aldous Huxley *Brave New World* 0 582 06016 8
Robin Jenks *The Cone-Gatherers* 0 582 06017 6
Doris Lessing *The Fifth Child* 0 582 06021 4
Joan Lindsay *Picnic at Hanging Rock* 0 582 08174 2
Bernard MacLaverty *Lamb* 0 582 06557 7
Brian Moore *Lies of Silence* 0 582 08170 X
George Orwell *Animal Farm* 0 582 06010 9
F Scott Fitzgerald *The Great Gatsby* 0 582 06023 0
Robert Swindells *Daz 4 Zoe* 0 582 30243 9
Anne Tyler *A Slipping-Down Life* 0 582 29247 6
Virginia Woolf *To the Lighthouse* 0 582 09714 2

Post-1914 Short Stories

Angelou, Goodison, Senior & Walker *Quartet of Stories* 0 582 28730 8
Stan Barstow *The Human Element and Other Stories* 0 582 23369 0
Roald Dahl *A Roald Dahl Selection* 0 582 22281 8
selected by Geoff Barton *Stories Old and New* 0 582 28931 9
selected by Madhu Bhinda *Stories from Africa* 0 582 25393 4
        Stories from Asia 0 582 03922 3
selected by Celeste Flower *Mystery and Horror* 0 582 28928 9
selected by Jane Christopher *War Stories* 0 582 28927 0
selected by Susan Hill *Ghost Stories* 0 582 02261 X
selected by Beverley Naidoo, *Global Tales* 0 582 28929 7
Christine Donovan & Alun Hicks
selected by Andrew Whittle & *Ten D H Lawrence Short Stories* 0 582 29249 2
Roy Blatchford

Post-1914 Poetry

collected & edited by Roy Blatchford *Voices of the Great War* 0 582 29248 4
edited by George MacBeth *Poetry 1900-1975* 0 582 35149 9
edited by Julia Markus & Paul Jordan *Poems 2* 0 582 25401 9

Post-1914 Plays

Alan Ayckbourn *Absent Friends* 0 582 30242 0
Terrence Rattigan *The Winslow Boy* 0 582 06019 2
Jack Rosenthal *P'Tang, Yang, Kipperbang and other TV Plays* 0 582 22389 X
Willy Russell *Educating Rita* 0 582 06013 3
        Shirley Valentine 0 582 08173 4
selected by Geoff Barton *Ten Short Plays* 0 582 25383 7
selected by Michael Marland *Scenes from Plays* 0 582 25394 2
Peter Shaffer *The Royal Hunt of the Sun* 0 582 06014 1
        Equus 0 582 09712 6
Bernard Shaw *Pygmalion* 0 582 06015 X
        Saint Joan 0 582 07786 9
Sheridan, Richard Brinsley *The Rivals/The School for Scandal* 0 582 25396 9

Contents

Introduction   vii

    Poems – soft or hard?   vii
    How to read a poem   viii

Maya Angelou   I

    About the poet   I

    Coleridge Jackson   2
    Artful Pose   4
    When I Think about Myself   5
    Still I Rise   6
    Phenomenal Woman   8
    Weekend Glory   10
    Woman Work   12
    On Aging   13
    Momma Welfare Roll   14
    The Lie   15
    Prescience   16

Philip Larkin   17

    About the poet   17

    Next, Please   19
    I Remember, I Remember   20
    Wild Oats   22
    Reasons for Attendance   23
    Annus Mirabilis   24
    Poetry of Departures   25
    The View   26
    Posterity   27

CONTENTS

Toads   28
Home Is So Sad   29
Mr Bleaney   30
An Arundel Tomb   32

U. A. Fanthorpe   34

About the poet   34

Growing Up   35
Growing Out   37
Half-past Two   39
Reports   41
You Will Be Hearing from Us Shortly   43
Dictator   45
Old Man, Old Man   46
After Visiting Hours   47
Casehistory: Alison (head injury)   49
Patients   50
Going Under   52

Sylvia Plath   53

About the poet   53

Mushrooms   55
Metaphors   56
You're   57
Morning Song   58
Blackberrying   59
Mirror   61
The Bee Meeting   62
The Arrival of the Bee Box   65
Stings   66
Wintering   69

CONTENTS

Seamus Heaney 71

About the poet 71

Singing School: 2 A Constable Calls 72
Death of a Naturalist 73
Blackberry-Picking 75
Mid-Term Break 76
The Grauballe Man 77
Punishment 79
Act of Union 81
Changes 82
Seeing Things (I) 83
Field of Vision 84
Wheels within Wheels 85

Anne Stevenson 87

About the poet 87

In the Nursery 88
The Victory 88
Hands 89
The Marriage 91
from Correspondences:
   A daughter's difficulties as a wife 92
   Fragments 97
   A blunder rectified 99
From the Motorway 100
Terrorist 102
Black Hole 103
Bloody Bloody 104

James Fenton 106

About the poet 106

The Skip 107
Hinterhof 110

CONTENTS

Nothing   111
Serious   112
Out of Danger   113
For Andrew Wood   114
I Saw a Child   116
Tiananmen   118
Here Come the Drum Majorettes!   120

Carol Ann Duffy   124

About the poet   124

Away and See   125
Comprehensive   126
Welltread   128
The Good Teachers   129
In Mrs Tilscher's Class   130
Human Interest   131
Saying Something   132
Valentine   133
Mrs Skinner, North Street   134
War Photographer   135
Deportation   136
Yes, Officer   137

Glossary: reading the poems   138

Technical terms   148

Study programme   150

Introduction

Poems – soft or hard?

Why does the thought of poetry make many people groan? When you think of the word 'poet' do you think of some soft, dreamy romantic, out of touch with the real world? Perhaps you could blame those rhymes inside birthday and Christmas cards, that just sound slushy and don't *mean* much? We hope that you will find that the poems in this book are not like that. We like them because we think that they are exact and precise and true. See if you agree with us as you read them.

Not many of them are about flowers, but they are a bit like flowers. Not because flowers are pretty, but because flowers are complicated structures which have evolved to carry out a task, the task of reproducing the plant they grow on. Poems are also complicated structures which reproduce things, but in their case what they reproduce are the observations, thoughts and emotions which led the poet to write the poem. If the poem works well, these observations, thoughts and emotions will be reproduced in you. Just as every bit of the flower – the petals, sepals, pollen, scent and so on – has a function, so every bit of a poem – the ideas, the choice of words, their sounds, their rhythms, the rhymes, the imagery – has a function. The function is to convey a precise meaning to you, the reader. And just like the flower, the poem may also be beautiful.

Bearing this in mind, a poem invites a different sort of reading from prose. We need to read a poem not just from beginning to end but around and across, getting a feel for its shape on the page – viewing the flower from every angle. There may be patterns of ideas, words and sounds that create echoes within the poem and encourage your eye and ear to roam backwards and forwards over the lines and the spaces between them – showing off the flower at its best. So how do you start?

How to read a poem

Looking at one poem in detail may give you an idea of how you could approach others for yourself. To do this, follow the step-by-step method outlined below.

☐ Read the poem to yourself a couple of times. If you have the opportunity, read it aloud or listen to a reading of it. If not, make sure you read it aloud to yourself in your head so you get a feel for the sounds, including the rhythms, that the poet has been playing with.

☐ Now jot down your first impressions of the poem on a piece of paper, in any order. Don't worry if you feel you don't understand it – just aim to capture anything the poem makes you think or feel.

Try doing this yourself with 'Welltread' by Carol Ann Duffy.

Welltread

Welltread was Head and the Head's face was a fist. Yes,
I've got him. Spelling and Punishment. A big brass bell
dumb on his desk till only he shook it, and children
ran shrieking in the locked yard. Mr Welltread. Sir.

He meant well. They all did then. The loud, inarticulate dads,
the mothers who spat on hankies and rubbed you away.
But Welltread looked like a gangster. Welltread stalked
the forms, collecting thruppenny bits in a soft black hat.

We prayed for Aberfan, vaguely reprieved. My socks dissolved,
two grey pools at my ankles, at the shock of my name
called out. The memory brings me to my feet
as a foul would. The wrong child for a trite crime.

And all I could say was No. Welltread straightened my hand
as though he could read the future there, then hurt himself
more than he hurt me. There was no cause for complaint.
There was the burn of a cane in my palm, still smouldering.

Now read what one student wrote:

> *Child caned on hand for something she didn't do. Welltread sounds terrifying, first line makes you feel you couldn't argue with him. No escape from 'locked yard'. Person writing is adult now, looking back. She's 'still smouldering'. Sometimes goes back to her talking like the child 'Mr Welltread. Sir'. That's good – makes you feel you are there. Reminds me of time I got done for writing on desk. What's Aberfan?*

3 At this point it would be useful to share your first impressions with someone else or a small group. This will help you in two ways. First, you will understand more clearly what you think by expressing your thoughts; second, you will learn from hearing how other people have reacted to the poem.

4 Now is the time to return to the poem and think in more detail about your response. Here are some questions which may help to direct and develop your thoughts. It is often useful to write notes around the poem itself at this stage as well as separately.

a) What is the poem about? How does the poet want you to think/feel towards the poem's subject? How does it develop? Has the poet used the poem to move from one position to another or to expand on one experience? Can you link what it describes to your own experience?

b) Is the title appropriate? What clues does it give you as to the poem's meaning? Can you think of an alternative?

c) Who seems to be talking in the poem? What is the tone of voice and/or mood and does it change? How has the poet used sounds and rhythms to build up the voice or voices in the poem?

d) Are there any particular words or phrases which are striking? (You may want to mention symbols, images, metaphors and similes here – look them up in 'Technical terms' pages 148–9 if you are not sure what these words mean.) If you removed or replaced any words or phrases, what effect would it have?

e) Does the way the words are laid out on the page seem important? Is the length of the verses, lines, sentences important? Try changing these around: what difference does it make?

f) Are there any patterns in the poem that you've noticed: repeated ideas, images, words, phrases or sounds? (You might want to refer to alliteration and assonance here – look them up in 'Technical terms' if you are not sure what these words mean.)

g) Are there any questions you would like to ask the poet about the poem? What do you think their aims were and how successful do you think they have been?

h) Rereading the poem as a whole again, are there any further notes you would like to make? Have your first impressions changed?

This is what the same student wrote on 'Welltread': the sections correspond to the steps outlined above.

a) *About Head, wants to recreate what he was like and fear he made children feel. Talks about his general behaviour and appearance and then focuses on particular incident with narrator. I can remember similar feelings of confusion, anger, lack of power as a child.*

b) *Title interesting, shows Welltread focus of poem, commanding power even from head of poem. Interesting there's no 'Mr'. Must have been what he was called by children.*

c) *Child now adult talking – good movement back into voice of child, bringing past alive. 'Mr Welltread. Sir.' Short sentences help it sound real/dramatic. Sometimes uses phrases adults use at times: 'He meant well', 'then hurt himself/more than he hurt me', both undercut by pain he caused.*

d) *Whole first line full of impact, emphasised by monosyllables. Metaphor 'face was a fist' helped by alliteration with 'f'. 'Yes,/*

'I've got him' refers not only to having him teach her but also that she's caught him successfully in the words of the poem — link between learning and being punished very clear with 'Spelling and Punishment' in second line. Also, little details, e.g. 'till only he shook it' of bell — 'only' conveys whole world of threats if anyone else dared shake it; e.g. only describing socks when shocked by name, rather than feelings, catches the fact that she must have had to jump up quickly and in fear, also sense of losing hold. 'No' stressed — only protest. Last line good because hurt of punishment 'still smouldering' as an adult. Alliteration adds to way last line echoes in mind.

e) *Each verse extends detail of Welltread and her experience of him. Short sentences and broken lines can add to sense of lived past, also give feeling of narrator recollecting bit by bit.*

f) *Repeating his name emphasises his dominance already stated by title, almost becomes like accusing chant. Moving in and out of past as experienced and reflected on — already mentioned sounds — alliteration in first and last verse already mentioned.*

g) *Was it really his name or did she make it up for poem? How were her earlier drafts different from the final version? Aim was to build up picture of him and effect he had on her. Very successful.*

h) *See more clearly how the poem's built up now, first showing Head and then how she's involved with him.*

5 Once you have thought about the poems in detail you may want to share your thoughts again with a partner or small group.

Next you may need to focus your ideas in order to present them to another audience. In Section 1 of the 'Study programme' (pages 150–72) you will find a range of approaches developed in relation to specific poems. These can be adapted or altered to suit other poems. You will also find suggestions for working on two or three poems on similar themes by the same poet, such as Sylvia Plath's poems on bees, James Fenton's poems on politics and war, and U. A. Fanthorpe's poems about patients in hospital. Sorting out the similarities and differences between them should help you clarify your ideas on individual poems. Section 2 of the 'Study programme' (pages 173–5) offers thematic approaches to looking at the poems, and Section 3 (page 176) provides further general ideas for exploring a poet or a set of poems: these may also be useful as a means of focusing on individual poems.

Maya Angelou

About the poet

Maya Angelou has described her life as 'a roller coaster'. She was born in 1928 in St Louis, Missouri. At eight, she was raped by her mother's boy-friend; he was beaten to death by an angry mob the day after his trial and she became mute for five years. At sixteen, her son Guy was born. In order to support the two of them she embarked on a career which began with prostitution and involved, over the years, being a dancer, a singer, an actress, a cook, a Black activist, the editor of an Egyptian newspaper, a wife (three times), a playwright and eventually appointment to a lifetime post as Professor of American Studies at Wake College, North Carolina.

Her poetry radiates with the same resilient zest for life and strength of opinion that is found in her five volumes of autobiography. She draws on her own experiences but moves beyond them to offer reflections on race, gender, ageing, love and relationships, to which we can all relate. As she herself said:

> The scars are alive and you rub your pencil over them to sharpen it. That, for me, is what it means to write. But I rarely ask for sympathy; that's not my way. If a person thinks, then, possibly, a little of the gloom of ignorance is lifted from us. That's my real intent.

She has also said she writes for the voice, 'never for the page. Poetry is music for the voice; I hear the language when I write.'

Coleridge Jackson

Coleridge Jackson had nothing
to fear. He weighed sixty pounds
more than his sons and one
hundred pounds more than his wife.

His neighbors knew he wouldn't
take tea for the fever.
The gents at the poolroom
walked gently in his presence.

So everyone used
to wonder why,
when his puny boss, a little
white bag of bones and
squinty eyes, when he frowned
at Coleridge, sneered at
the way Coleridge shifted
a ton of canned goods from
the east wall of the warehouse
all the way to the west,
when that skimpy piece of
man-meat called Coleridge
a sorry nigger,
Coleridge kept his lips closed,
sealed, jammed tight.
Wouldn't raise his eyes,
held his head at a slant,
looking way off somewhere
else.

Everybody in the neighborhood wondered
why Coleridge would come home,
pull off his jacket, take off
his shoes, and beat the
water and the will out of his puny
little family.

Everybody, even Coleridge, wondered
(the next day, or even later that
same night).
Everybody. But the weasly little
sack-of-bones boss with his
envious little eyes,
he knew. He always
knew. And
when people told him about
Coleridge's family, about the
black eyes and the bruised
faces, the broken bones,
Lord, how that scrawny man
grinned.

And the next
day, for a few hours, he treated
Coleridge nice. Like Coleridge
had just done him the biggest
old favor. Then, right
after lunch, he'd start on
Coleridge again.

'Here, Sambo, come here.
Can't you move any faster
than that? Who on earth
needs a lazy nigger?'
And Coleridge would just
stand there. His eyes sliding
away, lurking at something else.

Artful Pose

Of falling leaves and melting
snows, of birds
in their delights
Some poets sing
their melodies
tendering my nights
sweetly.

My pencil halts
and will not go
along that quiet path
I need to write
of lovers false

and hate
and hateful wrath
quickly.

When I Think about Myself

When I think about myself,
I almost laugh myself to death,
My life has been one great big joke,
A dance that's walked
A song that's spoke,
I laugh so hard I almost choke
When I think about myself.

Sixty years in these folks' world
The child I works for calls me girl
I say 'Yes ma'am' for working's sake.
Too proud to bend
Too poor to break,
I laugh until my stomach ache,
When I think about myself.

My folks can make me split my side,
I laughed so hard I nearly died,
The tales they tell, sound just like lying,
They grow the fruit,
But eat the rind,
I laugh until I start to crying,
When I think about my folks.

Still I Rise

You may write me down in history
With your bitter, twisted lies,
You may trod me in the very dirt
But still, like dust, I'll rise.

Does my sassiness upset you?
Why are you beset with gloom?
'Cause I walk like I've got oil wells
Pumping in my living room.

Just like moons and like suns,
With the certainty of tides,
Just like hopes springing high,
Still I'll rise.

Did you want to see me broken?
Bowed head and lowered eyes?
Shoulders falling down like teardrops,
Weakened by my soulful cries.

Does my haughtiness offend you?
Don't you take it awful hard
'Cause I laugh like I've got gold mines
Diggin' in my own back yard.

You may shoot me with your words,
You may cut me with your eyes,
You may kill me with your hatefulness,
But still, like air, I'll rise.

Does my sexiness upset you?
Does it come as a surprise
That I dance like I've got diamonds
At the meeting of my thighs?

Out of the huts of history's shame
I rise
Up from a past that's rooted in pain
I rise
I'm a black ocean, leaping and wide,
Welling and swelling I bear in the tide.

Leaving behind nights of terror and fear
I rise
Into a daybreak that's wondrously clear
I rise
Bringing the gifts that my ancestors gave,
I am the dream and the hope of the slave.
I rise
I rise
I rise.

Phenomenal Woman

Pretty women wonder where my secret lies.
I'm not cute or built to suit a fashion model's size
But when I start to tell them,
They think I'm telling lies.
I say,
It's in the reach of my arms,
The span of my hips,
The stride of my step,
The curl of my lips.
I'm a woman
Phenomenally.
Phenomenal woman,
That's me.

I walk into a room
Just as cool as you please,
And to a man,
The fellows stand or
Fall down on their knees.
Then they swarm around me,
A hive of honey bees.
I say,
It's the fire in my eyes,
And the flash of my teeth,
The swing in my waist,
And the joy in my feet.
I'm a woman
Phenomenally.
Phenomenal woman,
That's me.

Men themselves have wondered
What they see in me.
They try so much
But they can't touch
My inner mystery.
When I try to show them
They say they still can't see.
I say,
It's in the arch of my back,
The sun of my smile,
The ride of my breasts,
The grace of my style.
I'm a woman
Phenomenally.
Phenomenal woman,
That's me.

Now you understand
Just why my head's not bowed.
I don't shout or jump about
Or have to talk real loud.
When you see me passing
It ought to make you proud.
I say,
It's in the click of my heels,
The bend of my hair,
The palm of my hand,
The need for my care.
'Cause I'm a woman
Phenomenally.
Phenomenal woman,
That's me.

Weekend Glory

Some dichty folks
don't know the facts,
posin' and preenin'
and puttin' on acts,
stretchin' their necks
and strainin' their backs.

They move into condos
up over the ranks,
pawn their souls
to the local banks.
Buying big cars
they can't afford,
ridin' around town
actin' bored.

If they want to learn how to live life right,
they ought to study me on Saturday night.

My job at the plant
ain't the biggest bet,
but I pay my bills
and stay out of debt.
I get my hair done
for my own self's sake,
so I don't have to pick
and I don't have to rake.

Take the church money out
and head cross town
to my friend girl's house
where we plan our round.
We meet our men and go to a joint
where the music is blues
and to the point.

Folks write about me.
They just can't see
how I work all week
at the factory.
Then get spruced up
and laugh and dance
And turn away from worry
with sassy glance.

They accuse me of livin'
from day to day,
but who are they kiddin'?
So are they.

My life ain't heaven
but it sure ain't hell.
I'm not on top
but I call it swell
if I'm able to work
and get paid right
and have the luck to be Black
on a Saturday night.

Woman Work

I've got the children to tend
The clothes to mend
The floor to mop
The food to shop
Then the chicken to fry
The baby to dry
I got company to feed
The garden to weed
I've got the shirts to press
The tots to dress
The cane to be cut
I gotta clean up this hut
Then see about the sick
And the cotton to pick.

Shine on me, sunshine
Rain on me, rain
Fall softly, dewdrops
And cool my brow again.

Storm, blow me from here
With your fiercest wind
Let me float across the sky
'Til I can rest again.

Fall gently, snowflakes
Cover me with white
Cold icy kisses and
Let me rest tonight.

Sun, rain, curving sky
Mountain, oceans, leaf and stone
Star shine, moon glow
You're all that I can call my own.

On Aging

When you see me sitting quietly,
Like a sack left on the shelf,
Don't think I need your chattering.
I'm listening to myself.
Hold! Stop! Don't pity me!
Hold! Stop your sympathy!
Understanding if you got it,
Otherwise I'll do without it!

When my bones are stiff and aching
And my feet won't climb the stair,
I will only ask one favor:
Don't bring me no rocking chair.

When you see me walking, stumbling,
Don't study and get it wrong.
'Cause tired don't mean lazy
And every goodbye ain't gone.
I'm the same person I was back then,
A little less hair, a little less chin,
A lot less lungs and much less wind.
But ain't I lucky I can still breathe in.

Momma Welfare Roll

Her arms semaphore fat triangles,
Pudgy hands bunched on layered hips
Where bones idle under years of fatback
And lima beans.
Her jowls shiver in accusation
Of crimes clichéd by
Repetition. Her children, strangers
To childhood's toys, play
Best the games of darkened doorways,
Rooftop tag, and know the slick feel of
Other people's property.

Too fat to whore,
Too mad to work,
Searches her dreams for the
Lucky sign and walks bare-handed
Into a den of bureaucrats for
Her portion.
'They don't give me welfare.
I take it.'

The Lie

Today, you threaten to leave me.
I hold curses, in my mouth,
which could flood your path, sear
bottomless chasms in your road.

I keep, behind my lips,
invectives capable of tearing
the septum from your
nostrils and the skin from your back.

Tears, copious as a spring rain,
are checked in ducts
and screams are crowded in a corner
of my throat.

You are leaving?

Aloud, I say:
I'll help you pack, but it's getting late,
I have to hurry or miss my date.
When I return, I know you'll be gone.
Do drop a line or telephone.

Prescience

Had I known that the heart
breaks slowly, dismantling itself
into unrecognizable plots of
misery,

Had I known the heart would leak,
slobbering its sap, with a vulgar
visibility, into the dressed-up
dining rooms of strangers,

Had I known that solitude could
stifle the breath, loosen the joint,
and force the tongue against the
palate,

Had I known that loneliness could
keloid, winding itself around the
body in an ominous and beautiful
cicatrix,

Had I known yet I would have loved
you, your brash and insolent beauty,
your heavy comedic face
and knowledge of sweet
delights,

But from a distance
I would have left you whole and wholly
for the delectation of those who
wanted more and cared less.

Philip Larkin

About the poet

Philip Larkin was born in 1922, which makes him the first-born of the poets included in this volume. He wrote very little compared to some other poets. He published just three slim volumes at approximately ten-year intervals after he discovered his characteristic 'voice' some time in the late 1940s: *The Less Deceived* (1955), *The Whitsun Weddings* (1965) and *High Windows* (1974). After this he wrote little, feeling that poetry had 'given him up'. He died in 1985. Despite this small output, his reputation has grown steadily. 'Larkin now seems to dominate the history of English poetry in the second half of the twentieth century', Blake Morrison wrote in *The Oxford Companion to Twentieth Century Poetry* (1994).

Larkin came from a respectable middle-class background. His father was town treasurer of Coventry. Larkin deals with his uneventful childhood in 'I Remember, I Remember'. He won a scholarship to St John's College, Oxford. He was unfit to serve in the forces in the Second World War, so became a librarian in Wellington, Shropshire instead. These early experiences form the background of his two novels, *Jill* (1946) and *A Girl in Winter* (1947).

His early poems, on his own estimation, relied too much on imitating the style of other poets he admired. It was not until about 1950 that he developed the 'voice' — 'plain-speaking, sceptical, modest, unshowy, awkward, commonsensical, even rather dry and dull' according to Blake Morrison — that unites all the poems collected in this volume. Larkin's poems seem to follow a train of thought, reaching a tentative conclusion which strikes the reader as honest because

17

of its very lack of certainty. If Larkin concludes a poem with a grand statement such as 'What will survive of us is love' ('An Arundel Tomb') he precedes it by calling it an 'almost instinct' which is only 'almost true'.

Although Larkin wrote on many subjects both public and personal, the poems we have selected here deal mainly with his own life: his childhood, love-life, work, home, reputation and death. The tone of the poems is often sad and sombre. We are led to feel that most things will end in failure, but the vein of ironic, grim humour that runs below the despair makes reading the poems anything but depressing. Whether at his most plain-spoken and forceful as in 'Poetry of Departures' or his most complex and meditative as in 'An Arundel Tomb', reading Larkin's poems can be a rich and enjoyable experience.

Next, Please

Always too eager for the future, we
Pick up bad habits of expectancy.
Something is always approaching; every day
Till then we say,

Watching from a bluff the tiny, clear,
Sparkling armada of promises draw near.
How slow they are! And how much time they waste,
Refusing to make haste!

Yet still they leave us holding wretched stalks
Of disappointment, for, though nothing balks
Each big approach, leaning with brasswork prinked,
Each rope distinct,

Flagged, and the figurehead with golden tits
Arching our way, it never anchors; it's
No sooner present than it turns to past.
Right to the last

We think each one will heave to and unload
All good into our lives, all we are owed
For waiting so devoutly and so long.
But we are wrong:

Only one ship is seeking us, a black-
Sailed unfamiliar, towing at her back
A huge and birdless silence. In her wake
No waters breed or break.

I Remember, I Remember

Coming up England by a different line
For once, early in the cold new year,
We stopped, and, watching men with number-plates
Sprint down the platform to familiar gates,
'Why, Coventry!' I exclaimed. 'I was born here.'

I leant far out , and squinnied for a sign
That this was still the town that had been 'mine'
So long, but found I wasn't even clear
Which side was which. From where those cycle-crates
Were standing, had we annually departed

For all those family hols? . . . A whistle went:
Things moved. I sat back, staring at my boots.
'Was that,' my friend smiled, 'where you "have your
    roots"?'
No, only where my childhood was unspent,
I wanted to retort, just where I started:

By now I've got the whole place clearly charted.
Our garden, first: where I did not invent
Blinding theologies of flowers and fruits,
And wasn't spoken to by an old hat.
And here we have that splendid family

I never ran to when I got depressed,
The boys all biceps and the girls all chest,
Their comic Ford, their farm where I could be
'Really myself'. I'll show you, come to that,
The bracken where I never trembling sat,

Determined to go through with it; where she
Lay back, and 'all became a burning mist'.
And, in those offices, my doggerel
Was not set up in blunt ten-point, nor read
By a distinguished cousin of the mayor,

Who didn't call and tell my father *There
Before us, had we the gift to see ahead* –
'You look as if you wished the place in Hell,'
My friend said, 'judging from your face.' 'Oh well,
I suppose it's not the place's fault,' I said.

'Nothing, like something, happens anywhere.'

Wild Oats

About twenty years ago
Two girls came in where I worked –
A bosomy English rose
And her friend in specs I could talk to.
Faces in those days sparked
The whole shooting-match off, and I doubt
If ever one had like hers:
But it was the friend I took out,

And in seven years after that
Wrote over four hundred letters,
Gave a ten-guinea ring
I got back in the end, and met
At numerous cathedral cities
Unknown to the clergy. I believe
I met beautiful twice. She was trying
Both times (so I thought) not to laugh.

Parting, after about five
Rehearsals, was an agreement
That I was too selfish, withdrawn,
And easily bored to love.
Well, useful to get that learnt.
In my wallet are still two snaps
Of bosomy rose with fur gloves on.
Unlucky charms, perhaps.

Reasons for Attendance

The trumpet's voice, loud and authoritative,
Draws me a moment to the lighted glass
To watch the dancers – all under twenty-five –
Shifting intently, face to flushed face,
Solemnly on the beat of happiness.

– Or so I fancy, sensing the smoke and sweat,
The wonderful feel of girls. Why be out here?
But then, why be in there? Sex, yes, but what
Is sex? Surely, to think the lion's share
Of happiness is found by couples – sheer

Inaccuracy, as far as I'm concerned.
What calls me is that lifted, rough-tongued bell
(Art, if you like) whose individual sound
Insists I too am individual.
It speaks; I hear; others may hear as well,

But not for me, nor I for them; and so
With happiness. Therefore I stay outside,
Believing this; and they maul to and fro,
Believing that; and both are satisfied,
If no one has misjudged himself. Or lied.

Annus Mirabilis

Sexual intercourse began
In nineteen sixty-three
(Which was rather late for me) –
Between the end of the *Chatterley* ban
And the Beatles' first LP.

Up till then there'd only been
A sort of bargaining,
A wrangle for a ring,
A shame that started at sixteen
And spread to everything.

Then all at once the quarrel sank:
Everyone felt the same,
And every life became
A brilliant breaking of the bank,
A quite unlosable game.

So life was never better than
In nineteen sixty-three
(Though just too late for me) –
Between the end of the *Chatterley* ban
And the Beatles' first LP.

Poetry of Departures

Sometimes you hear, fifth-hand,
As epitaph:
He chucked up everything
And just cleared off,
And always the voice will sound
Certain you approve
This audacious, purifying,
Elemental move.

And they are right, I think.
We all hate home
And having to be there:
I detest my room,
Its specially-chosen junk,
The good books, the good bed,
And my life, in perfect order:
So to hear it said

He walked out on the whole crowd
Leaves me flushed and stirred,
Like *Then she undid her dress*
Or *Take that you bastard;*
Surely I can, if he did?
And that helps me stay
Sober and industrious.
But I'd go today,

Yes, swagger the nut-strewn roads,
Crouch in the fo'c'sle
Stubbly with goodness, if
It weren't so artificial,
Such a deliberate step backwards
To create an object:
Books; china; a life
Reprehensibly perfect.

The View

The view is fine from fifty,
    Experienced climbers say;
So, overweight and shifty,
    I turn to face the way
    That led me to this day.

Instead of fields and snowcaps
    And flowered lanes that twist,
The track breaks at my toe-caps
    And drops away in mist.
    The view does not exist.

Where has it gone, the lifetime?
    Search me. What's left is drear.
Unchilded and unwifed, I'm
    Able to view that clear:
    So final. And so near.

Posterity

Jake Balokowsky, my biographer,
Has this page microfilmed. Sitting inside
His air-conditioned cell at Kennedy
In jeans and sneakers, he's no call to hide
Some slight impatience with his destiny:
'I'm stuck with this old fart at last a year;

I wanted to teach school in Tel Aviv,
But Myra's folks' – he makes the money sign –
'Insisted I got tenure. When there's kids –'
He shrugs. 'It's stinking dead, the research line;
Just let me put this bastard on the skids,
I'll get a couple of semesters leave

To work on Protest Theater.' They both rise,
Make for the Coke dispenser. 'What's he like?
Christ, I just told you. Oh, you know the thing,
That crummy textbook stuff from Freshman Psych,
Not out of kicks or something happening –
One of those old-type *natural* fouled-up guys.'

Toads

Why should I let the toad *work*
   Squat on my life?
Can't I use my wit as a pitchfork
   And drive the brute off?

Six days of the week it soils
   With its sickening poison –
Just for paying a few bills!
   That's out of proportion.

Lots of folk live on their wits:
   Lecturers, lispers,
Losels, loblolly-men, louts –
   They don't end as paupers;

Lots of folk live up lanes
   With fires in a bucket,
Eat windfalls and tinned sardines –
   They seem to like it.

Their nippers have got bare feet,
   Their unspeakable wives
Are skinny as whippets – and yet
   No one actually *starves*.

Ah, were I courageous enough
   To shout *Stuff your pension!*
But I know, all too well, that's the stuff
   That dreams are made on:

For something sufficiently toad-like
    Squats in me, too;
Its hunkers are heavy as hard luck,
    And cold as snow,

And will never allow me to blarney
    My way to getting
The fame and the girl and the money
    All at one sitting.

I don't say, one bodies the other
    One's spiritual truth;
But I do say it's hard to lose either,
    When you have both.

Home Is So Sad

Home is so sad. It stays as it was left,
Shaped to the comfort of the last to go
As if to win them back. Instead, bereft
Of anyone to please, it withers so,
Having no heart to put aside the theft

And turn again to what it started as,
A joyous shot at how things ought to be,
Long fallen wide. You can see how it was:
Look at the pictures and the cutlery.
The music in the piano stool. That vase.

Mr Bleaney

'This was Mr Bleaney's room. He stayed
The whole time he was at the Bodies, till
They moved him.' Flowered curtains, thin and frayed,
Fall to within five inches of the sill,

Whose window shows a strip of building land,
Tussocky, littered. 'Mr Bleaney took
My bit of garden properly in hand.'
Bed, upright chair, sixty-watt bulb, no hook

Behind the door, no room for books or bags –
'I'll take it.' So it happens that I lie
Where Mr Bleaney lay, and stub my fags
On the same saucer-souvenir, and try

Stuffing my ears with cotton-wool, to drown
The jabbering set he egged her on to buy.
I know his habits - what time he came down,
His preference for sauce to gravy, why

He kept on plugging at the four aways –
Likewise their yearly frame: the Frinton folk
Who put him up for summer holidays,
And Christmas at his sister's house in Stoke.

But if he stood and watched the frigid wind
Tousling the clouds, lay on the fusty bed
Telling himself that this was home, and grinned,
And shivered, without shaking off the dread

That how we live measures our own nature,
And at his age having no more to show
Than one hired box should make him pretty sure
He warranted no better, I don't know.

An Arundel Tomb

Side by side, their faces blurred,
The earl and countess lie in stone,
Their proper habits vaguely shown
As jointed armour, stiffened pleat,
And that faint hint of the absurd –
The little dogs under their feet.

Such plainness of the pre-baroque
Hardly involves the eye, until
It meets his left-hand gauntlet, still
Clasped empty in the other; and
One sees, with a sharp tender shock,
His hand withdrawn, holding her hand.

They would not think to lie so long.
Such faithfulness in effigy
Was just a detail friends would see:
A sculptor's sweet commissioned grace
Thrown off in helping to prolong
The Latin names around the base.

They would not guess how early in
Their supine stationary voyage
The air would change to soundless damage,
Turn the old tenantry away;
How soon succeeding eyes begin
To look, not read. Rigidly they

Persisted, linked, through lengths and breadths
Of time. Snow fell, undated. Light
Each summer thronged the glass. A bright
Litter of birdcalls strewed the same
Bone-riddled ground. And up the paths
The endless altered people came,

Washing at their identity.
Now, helpless in the hollow of
An unarmorial age, a trough
Of smoke in slow suspended skeins
Above their scrap of history,
Only an attitude remains:

Time has transfigured them into
Untruth. The stone fidelity
They hardly meant has come to be
Their final blazon, and to prove
Our almost-instinct almost true:
What will survive of us is love.

☐ U.A. Fanthorpe

About the poet

A 'middle-aged drop-out' was how Ursula Fanthorpe described herself when 'poetry struck'. She had left a long career in English teaching, including several years as Head of English at Cheltenham Ladies College, to take a job as a hospital receptionist in Bristol. She was nearly fifty when her first poetry was published in 1978.

In 1980 she won third prize in the very large Observer/Arvon/South Bank Show poetry competition and this has been followed by writing scholarships and fellowships which have reflected her poetic talents more publicly. She has published five volumes of poetry: **Side Effects** (1978), **Standing To** (1982), **Voices Off** (1984), **A Watching Brief** (1987) and **Neck Verse** (1992). **Selected Poems** (1986) includes poems from the first three volumes.

Her work in the hospital provided a good observation post for many of her poems. These touch on concerns which run throughout much of her poetry, such as a focus on ordinary people, especially those who may not be able to speak out for themselves. You will find plenty of wit and humour along with the compassion she usually extends towards her subjects. She has said, 'I always mean there to be something below the surface but I do believe that by laughter you can get further than by doing a demolition job.'

Growing Up

I wasn't good
At being a baby. Burrowed my way
Through the long yawn of infancy,
Masking by instinct how much I knew
Of the senior world, sabotaging
As far as I could, biding my time,
Biting my rattle, my brother (in private),
Shoplifting daintily into my pram.
Not a good baby,
No.

I wasn't good
At being a child. I missed
The innocent age. Children,
Being childish, were beneath me.
Adults I despised or distrusted. They
Would label my every disclosure
Precocious, naïve, whatever it was.
I disdained definition, preferred to be surly.
Not a nice child,
No.

I wasn't good
At adolescence. There was a dance,
A catchy rhythm; I was out of step.
My body capered, nudging me
With hairy, fleshy growths and monthly outbursts,
To join the party. I tried to annul
The future, pretended I knew it already,

Was caught bloody-thighed, a criminal
Guilty of puberty.
Not a nice girl,
No.

(My hero, intransigent Emily,
Cauterized her own-dog-mauled
Arm with a poker,
Struggled to die on her feet,
Never told anyone anything.)

I wasn't good
At growing up. Never learned
The natives' art of life. Conversation
Disintegrated as I touched it,
So I played mute, wormed along years,
Reciting the hard-learned arcane litany
Of cliché, my company passport.
Not a nice person,
No.

The gift remains
Masonic, dark. But age affords
A vocation even for wallflowers.
Called to be connoisseur, I collect,
Admire, the effortless bravura
Of other people's lives, proper and comely,
Treading the measure, shopping, chaffing,
Quarrelling, drinking, not knowing
How right they are, or how, like well-oiled bolts,
Swiftly and sweet, they slot into the grooves
Their ancestors smoothed out along the grain.

Growing Out

We enter empty-handed, empty-hearted,
Freckled only by chromosomes and genes,
Novice-naked
(*Born on Monday*)

World, busy gossip, bustles up
Furnishing parents, a name,
A place in the sun
(*Christened on Tuesday*)

Parents erratically bombard us
With gifts – a rattle, love,
Uncles, words – tucking us in
To their particular nook.

The first growing out
Is easy. Bones shoot,
Teeth fall, appetites alter.
Parents officiate for us,
Handing down, or retailing
Through the columns of local papers.

Sometimes, if asked properly, they will
Deal with outmoded friends.

Growing out of parents
Is more expensive. Things
Of unquestioned presence –
A bed, a kettle, space –
Are suddenly unreliable;
They cost money.

We may also find we need
Someone to share them with
(*Married on Wednesday*)

These things, outgrown, become
Recriminatory. Best to consult
A specialist in division,
Who will slice accurately
Whatever is divisible:
House, money, children
(*Ill on Thursday*)

Finally we outgrow
Ourselves. Teeth and hair,
Being deciduous, drop;
Bones buckle and break;
Mind turns anarchist, body
Defects. Before long
We have grown out of everything
(*Worse on Friday*)

Free those who love you,
If you can, from posthumous
Distribution. Avoid
A cluttered end. Give
To the proper heirs before you go,
And celebrate your surrender
(*Died on Saturday*)

Grown out of all, you are now
Grown up. Empty-handed,
Empty-hearted, you have nothing
To hold you back
(*Buried on Sunday*)

Are ready to grow.

Half-past Two

Once upon a schooltime
He did Something Very Wrong
(I forget what it was).

And She said he'd done
Something Very Wrong, and must
Stay in the school-room till half-past two.

(Being cross, she'd forgotten
She hadn't taught him Time.
He was too scared at being wicked to remind her.)

He knew a lot of time: he knew
Gettinguptime, timeyouwereofftime,
Timetogohomenowtime, TVtime,

Timeformykisstime (that was Grantime).
All the important times he knew,
But not half-past two.

He knew the clockface, the little eyes
And two long legs for walking,
But he couldn't click its language,

So he waited, beyond onceupona,
Out of reach of all the timefors,
And knew he'd escaped for ever

Into the smell of old chrysanthemums on Her desk,
Into the silent noise his hangnail made,
Into the air outside the window, into ever.

And then, *My goodness,* she said,
Scuttling in, *I forgot all about you.*
Run along or you'll be late.

Reports

Has made a sound beginning
Strikes the right note:
Encouraging, but dull.
Don't give them anything
To take hold of. Even
Pronouns are dangerous.

The good have no history,
So don't bother. *Satisfactory*
Should satisfy them.

Fair and *Quite good,*
Multi-purpose terms,
By meaning nothing,
Apply to all.
Feel free to deploy them.

Be on your guard;
Unmanageable oaf cuts both ways.
Finds the subject difficult,
Acquitting you, converts
Oaf into idiot, usher to master.

Parent, child, head,
Unholy trinity, will read
Your scripture backwards.
Set them no riddles, just
Echo the common-room cliché:
Must make more effort.

Remember your high calling:
School is the world.
Born at *Sound beginning*,
We move from *Satisfactory*
To *Fair*, then *Find*
The subject difficult,
Learning at last we
Could have done better.

Stone only, final instructor,
Modulates from the indicative
With *Rest in peace*.

You Will Be Hearing from Us Shortly

You feel adequate to the demands of this position?
What qualities do you feel you
Personally have to offer?

                                                    Ah

Let us consider your application form.
Your qualifications, though impressive, are
Not, we must admit, precisely what
We had in mind. Would you care
To defend their relevance?

                                                    Indeed

Now your age. Perhaps you feel able
To make your own comment about that,
Too? We are conscious ourselves
Of the need for a candidate with precisely
The right degree of immaturity.

                                            So glad we agree

And now a delicate matter: your looks.
You do appreciate this work involves
Contact with the actual public? Might they,
Perhaps, find your appearance
Disturbing?

                                                Quite so

And your accent. That is the way
You have always spoken, is it? What
Of your education? Were
You educated? We mean, of course,
Where were you educated?

                   And how
Much of a handicap is that to you,
Would you say?

            Married, children,
We see. The usual dubious
Desire to perpetuate what had better
Not have happened at all. We do not
Ask what domestic disasters shimmer
Behind that vaguely unsuitable address.

And you were born – ?

                        Yes. Pity.

So glad we agree.

Dictator

He bestrides the wall-to-wall carpeting
Like a colossus. Imperiously
He surges from comma to semicolon.

Swaying in the throes of his passionate
Dictation, he creates little draughts,
Which stir my piles of flimsy paper.

If my phone rings, he answers
In an assumed accent.

Flexing the muscles of his mind,
He rides in triumph through the agendas
Of Area and District Management Committees,

Aborting all opposition with the flick
Of a fullstop. Laurelled and glossy,
He paces the colonnades of an imperial future,
With all his enemies liquidated.

When his letters are typed, he forgets to sign them.

Old Man, Old Man

He lives in a world of small recalcitrant
Things in bottles, with tacky labels. He was always
A man who did-it-himself.

Now his hands shamble among clues
He left for himself when he saw better,
And small things distress: *I've lost the hammer.*

Lifelong adjuster of environments,
Lord once of shed, garage and garden,
Each with its proper complement of tackle,

World authority on twelve different
Sorts of glue, connoisseur of nuts
And bolts, not good with daughters

But a dab hand with the Black and Decker,
Self-demoted in your nineties to washing-up
After supper, and missing crusted streaks

Of food on plates; have you forgotten
The jokes you no longer tell, as you forget
If you've smoked your timetabled cigarette?

Now television has no power to arouse
Your surliness; your wife could replace on the walls
Those pictures of disinherited children,

And you wouldn't know. Now you ramble
In your talk around London districts, fretting
At how to find your way from Holborn to Soho,

And where is Drury Lane? Old man, old man,
So obdurate in your contracted world,
Living in almost-dark, *I can see you,*

You said to me, *but only as a cloud.*
When I left, you tried not to cry. I love
Your helplessness, you who hate being helpless.

Let me find your hammer. Let me
Walk with you to Drury Lane. I am only a cloud.

After Visiting Hours

Like gulls they are still calling –
*I'll come again Tuesday. Our Dad
Sends his love.* They diminish, are gone.
Their world has received them,

As our world confirms us. Their debris
Is tidied into vases, lockers, minds.
We become pulses; mouthpieces
Of thermometers and bowels.

The trolley's rattle dispatches
The last lover. Now we can relax
Into illness, and reliably abstracted
Nurses will straighten our sheets,

Reorganize our symptoms. Outside,
Darkness descends like an eyelid.
It rains on our nearest and dearest
In car-parks, at bus-stops.

Now the bed-bound rehearse
Their repertoire of movements,
The dressing-gowned shuffle, clutching
Their glass bodies.

Now siren voices whisper
From headphones, and vagrant
Doctors appear, wreathed in stethoscopes
Like South Sea dancers.

All's well, all's quiet as the great
Ark noses her way into night,
Caulked, battened, blessed for her trip,
And behind, the gulls crying.

Casehistory: Alison (head injury)

(*She looks at her photograph*)

I would like to have known
My husband's wife, my mother's only daughter.
A bright girl she was.

Enmeshed in comforting
Fat, I wonder at her delicate angles.
Her autocratic knee

Like a Degas dancer's
Adjusts to the observer with airy poise,
That now lugs me upstairs

Hardly. Her face, broken
By nothing sharper than smiles, holds in its smiles
What I have forgotten.

She knows my father's dead,
And grieves for it, and smiles. She has digested
Mourning. Her smile shows it.

I, who need reminding
Every morning, shall never get over what
I do not remember.

Consistency matters.
I should like to keep faith with her lack of faith,
But forget her reasons.

Proud of this younger self,
I assert her achievements, her A levels,
Her job with a future.

Poor clever girl! I know,
For all my damaged brain, something she doesn't:
I am her future.

A bright girl she was.

Patients

Not the official ones, who have been
Diagnosed and made tidy. They are
The better sort of patient.

They know the answers to the difficult
Questions on the admission sheet
About religion, next of kin, sex.

They know the rules. The printed ones
In the *Guide for Patients*, about why we prefer
No smoking, the correct postal address;

Also the real ones, like the precise quota
Of servility each doctor expects,
When to have fits, and where to die.

These are not true patients. They know
Their way around, they present the right
Symptoms. But what can be done for us,

The undiagnosed? What drugs
Will help our Matron, whose cats are
Her old black husband and her young black son?

Who will prescribe for our nurses, fatally
Addicted to idleness and tea? What therapy
Will relieve our Psychiatrist of his lust

For young slim girls, who prudently
Pretend to his excitement, though age
Has freckled his hands and his breath smells old?

How to comfort our Director through his
Terminal distress, as he babbles of
Football and virility, trembling in sunlight?

There is no cure for us. O, if only
We could cherish our bizarre behaviour
With accurate clinical pity. But there are no

Notes to chart our journey, no one
Has even stamped CONFIDENTIAL or *Not to be
Taken out of the hospital* on our lives.

Going Under

I turn over pages, you say,
Louder than any woman in Europe.

But reading's my specific for keeping
Reality at bay; my lullaby.

You slip into sleep as fast
And neat as a dipper.
You lie there breathing, breathing.

My language is turn over
Over and over again. I am a fish
Netted on a giveaway mattress,
Urgent to be out of the air.

Reading would help; or pills.
But light would wake you from your resolute
Progress through night.

The dreams waiting for me twitter and bleat.
All the things I ever did wrong
Queue by the bed in order of precedence,
Worst last.

Exhausted by guilt, I nuzzle
Your shoulder. Out lobs
A casual, heavy arm. You anchor me
In your own easy sound.

Sylvia Plath

About the poet

Sylvia Plath was born in 1932 in Boston, Massachusetts. Her father was an immigrant from Germany. He was an expert on bees and taught at Boston University. He died when Plath was eight, and his loss was a source of much mental torment to her throughout her life. His ghost haunted her writing.

Plath did well at school and won scholarships first to a local college and then to Newnham College at Cambridge University. It was there that in 1956 she met and married Ted Hughes, the Yorkshire-born writer who became Poet Laureate in 1984. Their partnership as writers was very fertile: they struck sparks off each other and avidly read one another's drafts. The poetry of each of them grew in richness.

The relationship always had its stormy side, however, and in 1962 the couple split up following Plath's discovery that Hughes was having an affair. They were at this time living in a large, run-down old farm house in Devon. During October 1962, in time snatched from caring for her two young children, Plath produced an astonishing sequence of poems, including some of those collected in this book.

Sylvia Plath had a complex and troubled personality. She had attempted suicide in 1953, an incident which forms the centre of her autobiographical novel, *The Bell Jar* (published 1963). In December 1962 she moved to London, and in February 1963, in the middle of one of the coldest winters of the century, she killed herself.

Her first volume of poetry, **The Colossus**, was published in 1960. Her best-known poems were first published in **Ariel** in 1965. **Collected Poems**, edited and with an introduction by Ted Hughes, was published in 1981. Other volumes of letters to her mother and of short stories have also appeared.

Her poetry returns time after time to herself and her varying and sometimes extreme states of mind. Of the poems collected here, some, like 'Morning Song' and 'You're', are loving and affectionate. Others, like 'Mirror' or 'The Bee Meeting', deal with less positive emotions. What unites all her work is a feeling of intensity and restless intelligence.

Since her death her reputation has risen steadily. There have been many biographies and books about her poems, and the details of her life and death have been picked over obsessively by critics. She has been fancifully called the Marilyn Monroe of modern poetry, sharing as she does with the film star a brief, brilliant life and an early, controversial death by suicide. Her poems remain among the most powerful of recent times, retaining still a power to shock and intrigue the reader.

Mushrooms

Overnight, very
Whitely, discreetly,
Very quietly

Our toes, our noses
Take hold on the loam,
Acquire the air.

Nobody sees us,
Stops us, betrays us;
The small grains make room.

Soft fists insist on
Heaving the needles,
The leafy bedding,

Even the paving.
Our hammers, our rams,
Earless and eyeless,

Perfectly voiceless,
Widen the crannies,
Shoulder through holes. We

Diet on water,
On crumbs of shadow,
Bland-mannered, asking

Little or nothing.
So many of us!
So many of us!

We are shelves, we are
Tables, we are meek,
We are edible,

Nudgers and shovers
In spite of ourselves.
Our kind multiplies:

We shall by morning
Inherit the earth.
Our foot's in the door.

Metaphors

I'm a riddle in nine syllables,
An elephant, a ponderous house,
A melon strolling on two tendrils.
O red fruit, ivory, fine timbers!
This loaf's big with its yeasty rising.
Money's new-minted in this fat purse.
I'm a means, a stage, a cow in calf.
I've eaten a bag of green apples,
Boarded the train there's no getting off.

You're

Clownlike, happiest on your hands,
Feet to the stars, and moon-skulled,
Gilled like a fish. A common-sense
Thumbs-down on the dodo's mode.
Wrapped up in yourself like a spool,
Trawling your dark as owls do.
Mute as a turnip from the Fourth
Of July to All Fools' Day,
O high-riser, my little loaf.

Vague as fog and looked for like mail.
Farther off than Australia.
Bent-backed Atlas, our traveled prawn.
Snug as a bud and at home
Like a sprat in a pickle jug.
A creel of eels, all ripples.
Jumpy as a Mexican bean.
Right, like a well-done sum.
A clean slate, with your own face on.

Morning Song

Love set you going like a fat gold watch.
The midwife slapped your footsoles, and your bald cry
Took its place among the elements.

Our voices echo, magnifying your arrival. New statue.
In a drafty museum, your nakedness
Shadows our safety. We stand round blankly as walls.

I'm no more your mother
Than the cloud that distills a mirror to reflect its own
   slow
Effacement at the wind's hand.

All night your moth-breath
Flickers among the flat pink roses. I wake to listen:
A far sea moves in my ear.

One cry, and I stumble from bed, cow-heavy and floral
In my Victorian nightgown.
Your mouth opens clean as a cat's. The window square

Whitens and swallows its dull stars. And now you try
Your handful of notes;
The clear vowels rise like balloons.

Blackberrying

Nobody in the lane, and nothing, nothing but
    blackberries,
Blackberries on either side, though on the right mainly,
A blackberry alley, going down in hooks, and a sea
Somewhere at the end of it, heaving. Blackberries
Big as the ball of my thumb, and dumb as eyes
Ebon in the hedges, fat
With blue-red juices. These they squander on my
    fingers.
I had not asked for such a blood sisterhood; they must
    love me.
They accommodate themselves to my milkbottle,
    flattening their sides.

Overhead go the choughs in black, cacophonous
    flocks –
Bits of burnt paper wheeling in a blown sky.
Theirs is the only voice, protesting, protesting.
I do not think the sea will appear at all.
The high, green meadows are glowing, as if lit from
    within.
I come to one bush of berries so ripe it is a bush of flies,
Hanging their bluegreen bellies and their wing panes
    in a Chinese screen.
The honey-feast of the berries has stunned them;
    they believe in heaven.
One more hook, and the berries and bushes end.

The only thing to come now is the sea.
From between two hills a sudden wind funnels at me,
Slapping its phantom laundry in my face.
These hills are too green and sweet to have tasted salt.
I follow the sheep path between them. A last hook
      brings me
To the hills' northern face, and the face is orange rock
That looks out on nothing, nothing but a great space
Of white and pewter lights, and a din like silversmiths
Beating and beating at an intractable metal.

Mirror

I am silver and exact. I have no preconceptions.
Whatever I see I swallow immediately
Just as it is, unmisted by love or dislike.
I am not cruel, only truthful -
The eye of a little god, four-cornered.
Most of the time I meditate on the opposite wall.
It is pink, with speckles. I have looked at it so long
I think it is a part of my heart. But it flickers.
Faces and darkness separate us over and over.

Now I am a lake. A woman bends over me,
Searching my reaches for what she really is.
Then she turns to those liars, the candles or the moon.
I see her back, and reflect it faithfully.
She rewards me with tears and an agitation of hands.
I am important to her. She comes and goes.
Each morning it is her face that replaces the darkness.
In me she has drowned a young girl, and in me an old
    woman
Rises toward her day after day, like a terrible fish.

The Bee Meeting

Who are these people at the bridge to meet me?
    They are the villagers –
The rector, the midwife, the sexton, the agent for bees.
In my sleeveless summery dress I have no protection,
And they are all gloved and covered, why did nobody
    tell me?
They are smiling and taking out veils tacked to ancient
    hats..

I am nude as a chicken neck, does nobody love me?
Yes, here is the secretary of bees with her white shop
    smock,
Buttoning the cuffs at my wrists and the slit from my
    neck to my knees.
Now I am milkweed silk, the bees will not notice.
They will not smell my fear, my fear, my fear.

Which is the rector now, is it that man in black?
Which is the midwife, is that her blue coat?
Everybody is nodding a square black head, they are
    knights in visors,
Breastplates of cheesecloth knotted under the armpits.
Their smiles and their voices are changing. I am led
    through a beanfield.

Strips of tinfoil winking like people,
Feather dusters fanning their hands in a sea of bean
   flowers,
Creamy bean flowers with black eyes and leaves like
   bored hearts.
Is it blood clots the tendrils are dragging up that string?
No, no, it is scarlet flowers that will one day be edible.

Now they are giving me a fashionable white straw Italian
   hat
And a black veil that molds to my face, they are making
   me one of them.
They are leading me to the shorn grove, the circle of
   hives.
Is it the hawthorn that smells so sick?
The barren body of hawthorn, etherizing its children.

Is it some operation that is taking place?
It is the surgeon my neighbors are waiting for,
This apparition in a green helmet,
Shining gloves and white suit.
Is it the butcher, the grocer, the postman, someone I
   know?

I cannot run, I am rooted, and the gorse hurts me
With its yellow purses, its spiky armory.
I could not run without having to run forever.
The white hive is snug as a virgin,
Sealing off her brood cells, her honey, and quietly
   humming.

Smoke rolls and scarves in the grove.
The mind of the hive thinks this is the end of
     everything.
Here they come, the outriders, on their hysterical
     elastics.
If I stand very still, they will think I am cow-parsley,
A gullible head untouched by their animosity,

Not even nodding, a personage in a hedgerow.
The villagers open the chambers, they are hunting the
     queen.
Is she hiding, is she eating honey? She is very clever.
She is old, old, old, she must live another year, and she
     knows it.
While in their fingerjoint cells the new virgins

Dream of a duel they will win inevitably,
A curtain of wax dividing them from the bride flight,
The upflight of the murderess into a heaven that loves
     her.
The villagers are moving the virgins, there will be no
     killing.
The old queen does not show herself, is she so
     ungrateful?

I am exhausted, I am exhausted –
Pillar of white in a blackout of knives.
I am the magician's girl who does not flinch.
The villagers are untying their disguises, they are
     shaking hands.
Whose is that long white box in the grove, what have
     they accomplished, why am I cold.

The Arrival of the Bee Box

I ordered this, this clean wood box
Square as a chair and almost too heavy to lift.
I would say it was the coffin of a midget
Or a square baby
Were there not such a din in it.

The box is locked, it is dangerous.
I have to live with it overnight
And I can't keep away from it.
There are no windows, so I can't see what is in there.
There is only a little grid, no exit.

I put my eye to the grid.
It is dark, dark,
With the swarmy feeling of African hands
Minute and shrunk for export,
Black on black, angrily clambering.

How can I let them out?
It is the noise that appalls me most of all,
The unintelligible syllables.
It is like a Roman mob,
Small, taken one by one, but my god, together!

I lay my ear to furious Latin.
I am not a Caesar.
I have simply ordered a box of maniacs.
They can be sent back.
They can die, I need feed them nothing, I am the
    owner.

I wonder how hungry they are.
I wonder if they would forget me
If I just undid the locks and stood back and turned into
    a tree.
There is the laburnum, its blond colonnades,
And the petticoats of the cherry.

They might ignore me immediately
In my moon suit and funeral veil.
I am no source of honey
So why should they turn on me?
Tomorrow I will be sweet God, I will set them free.

The box is only temporary.

Stings

Bare-handed, I hand the combs.
The man in white smiles, bare-handed,
Our cheesecloth gauntlets neat and sweet,
The throats of our wrists brave lilies.
He and I

Have a thousand clean cells between us,
Eight combs of yellow cups,
And the hive itself a teacup,
White with pink flowers on it,
With excessive love I enameled it

Thinking 'Sweetness, sweetness'.
Brood cells gray as the fossils of shells
Terrify me, they seem so old.
What am I buying, wormy mahogany?
Is there any queen at all in it?

If there is, she is old,
Her wings torn shawls, her long body
Rubbed of its plush –
Poor and bare and unqueenly and even shameful.
I stand in a column

Of winged, unmiraculous women,
Honey-drudgers.
I am no drudge
Though for years I have eaten dust
And dried plates with my dense hair.

And seen my strangeness evaporate,
Blue dew from dangerous skin.
Will they hate me,
These women who only scurry,
Whose news is the open cherry, the open clover?

It is almost over.
I am in control.
Here is my honey-machine,
It will work without thinking,
Opening, in spring, like an industrious virgin

To scour the creaming crests
As the moon, for its ivory powders, scours the sea.
A third person is watching.
He has nothing to do with the bee-seller or with me.
Now he is gone

In eight great bounds, a great scapegoat.
Here is his slipper, here is another,
And here the square of white linen
He wore instead of a hat.
He was sweet,

The sweat of his efforts a rain
Tugging the world to fruit.
The bees found him out,
Molding onto his lips like lies,
Complicating his features.

They thought death was worth it, but I
Have a self to recover, a queen.
Is she dead, is she sleeping?
Where has she been,
With her lion-red body, her wings of glass?

Now she is flying
More terrible than she ever was, red
Scar in the sky, red comet
Over the engine that killed her –
The mausoleum, the wax house.

Wintering

This is the easy time, there is nothing doing.
I have whirled the midwife's extractor,
I have my honey,
Six jars of it,
Six cat's eyes in the wine cellar,

Wintering in a dark without window
At the heart of the house
Next to the last tenant's rancid jam
And the bottles of empty glitters –
Sir So-and-so's gin.

This is the room I have never been in.
This is the room I could never breathe in.
The black bunched in there like a bat,
No light
But the torch and its faint

Chinese yellow on appalling objects –
Black asininity. Decay.
Possession.
It is they who own me.
Neither cruel nor indifferent,

Only ignorant.
This is the time of hanging on for the bees – the bees
So slow I hardly know them,
Filing like soldiers
To the syrup tin

To make up for the honey I've taken.
Tate and Lyle keeps them going,
The refined snow.
It is Tate and Lyle they live on, instead of flowers.
They take it. The cold sets in.

Now they ball in a mass,
Black
Mind against all that white.
The smile of the snow is white.
It spreads itself out, a mile-long body of Meissen,

Into which, on warm days,
They can only carry their dead.
The bees are all women,
Maids and the long royal lady.
They have got rid of the men,

The blunt, clumsy stumblers, the boors.
Winter is for women –
The woman, still at her knitting,
At the cradle of Spanish walnut,
Her body a bulb in the cold and too dumb to think.

Will the hive survive, will the gladiolas
Succeed in banking their fires
To enter another year?
What will they taste of, the Christmas roses?
The bees are flying. They taste the spring.

Seamus Heaney

About the poet

Seamus Heaney was born into a Catholic farming family in County Derry, Northern Ireland in 1939. These bare facts identify him inevitably as a member of what he has called a 'tribe', and he has not shied away from examining the history of Ireland. He was educated at a school in Derry, and at Queen's University, Belfast, where he remained for six years as a teacher. In 1972 he moved south to the Republic of Ireland. He has become a poet with a firmly established international reputation ('Famous Seamus' to his friends!). He was Professor of Poetry at Oxford 1989–94.

Much of his earliest published poetry deals with his rural childhood. Later he became interested in the uncannily preserved Iron Age murder victims which have been found in peat bogs in northern Europe. They gave him a chance to think about tribal identity and violent death, subjects from which people from Northern Ireland find it hard to escape. Some poems have been written using the voice of Sweeney, a legendary King of Ulster, and he has translated Virgil and Dante. But his interest in history and literature has never led him away from the senses. He remains fascinated by the reality and physicality of the everyday world, recording facts and sensations plainly and vividly. The title of Heaney's 1991 collection, **Seeing Things**, plays with a simultaneous seeing of what is there now and the ghostly seed within it of the experience it will become in the memory.

Singing School

2   A Constable Calls

His bicycle stood at the window-sill,
The rubber cowl of a mud-splasher
Skirting the front mudguard,
Its fat black handlegrips

Heating in sunlight, the 'spud'
Of the dynamo gleaming and cocked back,
The pedal treads hanging relieved
Of the boot of the law.

His cap was upside down
On the floor, next his chair.
The line of its pressure ran like a bevel
In his slightly sweating hair.

He had unstrapped
The heavy ledger, and my father
Was making tillage returns
In acres, roods, and perches.

Arithmetic and fear.
I sat staring at the polished holster
With its buttoned flap, the braid cord
Looped into the revolver butt.

'Any other root crops?
Mangolds? Marrowstems? Anything like that?'
'No.' But was there not a line
Of turnips where the seed ran out

In the potato field? I assumed
Small guilts and sat
Imagining the black hole in the barracks.
He stood up, shifted the baton-case

Further round on his belt,
Closed the domesday book,
Fitted his cap back with two hands,
And looked at me as he said goodbye.

A shadow bobbed in the window.
He was snapping the carrier spring
Over the ledger. His boot pushed off
And the bicycle ticked, ticked, ticked.

Death of a Naturalist

All year the flax-dam festered in the heart
Of the townland; green and heavy headed
Flax had rotted there, weighted down by huge sods.
Daily it sweltered in the punishing sun.
Bubbles gargled delicately, bluebottles
Wove a strong gauze of sound around the smell.
There were dragon-flies, spotted butterflies,
But best of all was the warm thick slobber
Of frogspawn that grew like clotted water
In the shade of the banks. Here, every spring
I would fill jampotfuls of the jellied
Specks to range on window-sills at home,

On shelves at school, and wait and watch until
The fattening dots burst into nimble-
Swimming tadpoles. Miss Walls would tell us how
The daddy frog was called a bullfrog
And how he croaked and how the mammy frog
Laid hundreds of little eggs and this was
Frogspawn. You could tell the weather by frogs too
For they were yellow in the sun and brown
In rain.

    Then one hot day when fields were rank
With cowdung in the grass and angry frogs
Invaded the flax-dam; I ducked through hedges
To a coarse croaking that I had not heard
Before. The air was thick with a bass chorus.
Right down the dam gross-bellied frogs were cocked
On sods; their loose necks pulsed like sails. Some
    hopped:
The slap and plop were obscene threats. Some sat
Poised like mud grenades, their blunt heads farting.
I sickened, turned, and ran. The great slime kings
Were gathered there for vengeance and I knew
That if I dipped my hand the spawn would clutch it.

Blackberry-Picking

For Philip Hobsbaum

Late August, given heavy rain and sun
For a full week, the blackberries would ripen.
At first, just one, a glossy purple clot
Among others, red, green, hard as a knot.
You ate that first one and its flesh was sweet
Like thickened wine: summer's blood was in it
Leaving stains upon the tongue and lust for
Picking. Then red ones inked up and that hunger
Sent us out with milk-cans, pea-tins, jam-pots
Where briars scratched and wet grass bleached our
      boots.
Round hayfields, cornfields and potato-drills
We trekked and picked until the cans were full,
Until the tinkling bottom had been covered
With green ones, and on top big dark blobs burned
Like a plate of eyes. Our hands were peppered
With thorn pricks, our palms sticky as Bluebeard's.

We hoarded the fresh berries in the byre.
But when the bath was filled we found a fur,
A rat-grey fungus, glutting on our cache.
The juice was stinking too. Once off the bush
The fruit fermented, the sweet flesh would turn sour.
I always felt like crying. It wasn't fair
That all the lovely canfuls smelt of rot.
Each year I hoped they'd keep, knew they would not.

Mid-Term Break

I sat all morning in the college sick bay
Counting bells knelling classes to a close.
At two o'clock our neighbours drove me home.

In the porch I met my father crying –
He had always taken funerals in his stride –
And Big Jim Evans saying it was a hard blow.

The baby cooed and laughed and rocked the pram
When I came in, and I was embarrassed
By old men standing up to shake my hand

And tell me they were 'sorry for my trouble'.
Whispers informed strangers I was the eldest,
Away at school, as my mother held my hand

In hers and coughed out angry tearless sighs.
At ten o'clock the ambulance arrived
With the corpse, stanched and bandaged by the nurses.

Next morning I went up into the room. Snowdrops
And candles soothed the bedside; I saw him
For the first time in six weeks. Paler now,

Wearing a poppy bruise on his left temple,
He lay in the four foot box as in his cot.
No gaudy scars, the bumper knocked him clear.

A four foot box, a foot for every year.

The Grauballe Man

As if he had been poured
in tar, he lies
on a pillow of turf
and seems to weep

the black river of himself.
The grain of his wrists
is like bog oak,
the ball of his heel

like a basalt egg.
His instep has shrunk
cold as a swan's foot
or a wet swamp root.

His hips are the ridge
and purse of a mussel,
his spine an eel arrested
under a glisten of mud.

The head lifts,
the chin is a visor
raised above the vent
of his slashed throat

that has tanned and toughened.
The cured wound
opens inwards to a dark
elderberry place.

Who will say 'corpse'
to his vivid cast?
Who will say 'body'
to his opaque repose?

And his rusted hair,
a mat unlikely
as a foetus's.
I first saw his twisted face

in a photograph,
a head and shoulder
out of the peat,
bruised like a forceps baby,

but now he lies
perfected in my memory,
down to the red horn
of his nails,

hung in the scales
with beauty and atrocity:
with the Dying Gaul
too strictly compassed

on his shield,
with the actual weight
of each hooded victim,
slashed and dumped.

Punishment

I can feel the tug
of the halter at the nape
of her neck, the wind
on her naked front.

It blows her nipples
to amber beads,
it shakes the frail rigging
of her ribs.

I can see her drowned
body in the bog,
the weighing stone,
the floating rods and boughs.

Under which at first
she was a barked sapling
that is dug up
oak-bone, brain-firkin:

her shaved head
like a stubble of black corn,
her blindfold a soiled bandage,
her noose a ring

to store
the memories of love.
Little adulteress,
before they punished you

you were flaxen-haired,
undernourished, and your
tar-black face was beautiful.
My poor scapegoat,

I almost love you
but would have cast, I know,
the stones of silence.
I am the artful voyeur

of your brain's exposed
and darkened combs,
your muscles' webbing
and all your numbered bones:

I who have stood dumb
when your betraying sisters,
cauled in tar,
wept by the railings,

who would connive
in civilized outrage
yet understand the exact
and tribal, intimate revenge.

Act of Union

I

Tonight, a first movement, a pulse,
As if the rain in bogland gathered head
To slip and flood: a bog-burst,
A gash breaking open the ferny bed.
Your back is a firm line of eastern coast
And arms and legs are thrown
Beyond your gradual hills. I caress
The heaving province where our past has grown.
I am the tall kingdom over your shoulder
That you would neither cajole nor ignore.
Conquest is a lie. I grow older
Conceding your half-independent shore
Within whose borders now my legacy
Culminates inexorably.

II

And I am still imperially
Male, leaving you with the pain,
The rending process in the colony,
The battering ram, the boom burst from within.
The act sprouted an obstinate fifth column
Whose stance is growing unilateral.
His heart beneath your heart is a wardrum
Mustering force. His parasitical
And ignorant little fists already
Beat at your borders and I know they're cocked
At me across the water. No treaty
I foresee will salve completely your tracked
And stretchmarked body, the big pain
That leaves you raw, like opened ground, again.

Changes

As you came with me in silence
to the pump in the long grass

I heard much that you could not hear:
the bite of the spade that sank it,

the slithering and grumble
as the mason mixed his mortar,

and women coming with white buckets
like flashes on their ruffled wings.

The cast-iron rims of the lid
clinked as I uncovered it,

something stirred in its mouth.
I had a bird's eye view of a bird,

finch-green, speckly white,
nesting on dry leaves, flattened, still,

suffering the light.
So I roofed the citadel

as gently as I could, and told you
and you gently unroofed it

but where was the bird now?
There was a single egg, pebbly white,

and in the rusted bend of the spout
tail feathers splayed and sat tight.

So tender, I said, 'Remember this.
It will be good for you to retrace this path

when you have grown away and stand at last
at the very centre of the empty city.'

Seeing Things

I

Inishbofin on a Sunday morning.
Sunlight, turfsmoke, seagulls, boatslip, diesel.
One by one we were being handed down
Into a boat that dipped and shilly-shallied
Scaresomely every time. We sat tight
On short cross-benches, in nervous twos and threes,
Obedient, newly close, nobody speaking
Except the boatman, as the gunwales sank
And seemed they might ship water any minute.
The sea was very calm but even so,
When the engine kicked and our ferryman
Swayed for balance, reaching for the tiller,
I panicked at the shiftiness and heft
Of the craft itself. What guaranteed us -
That quick response and buoyancy and swim -
Kept me in agony. All the time
As we went sailing evenly across
The deep, still, seeable-down-into water,
It was as if I looked from another boat
Sailing through air, far up, and could see
How riskily we fared into the morning,
And loved in vain our bare, bowed, numbered heads.

Field of Vision

I remember this woman who sat for years
In a wheelchair, looking straight ahead
Out the window at sycamore trees unleafing
And leafing at the far end of the lane.

Straight out past the TV in the corner,
The stunted, agitated hawthorn bush,
The same small calves with their backs to wind and
    rain,
The same acre of ragwort, the same mountain.

She was steadfast as the big window itself.
Her brow was clear as the chrome bits of the chair.
She never lamented once and she never
Carried a spare ounce of emotional weight.

Face to face with her was an education
Of the sort you got across a well-braced gate –
One of those lean, clean, iron, roadside ones
Between two whitewashed pillars, where you could see

Deeper into the country than you expected
And discovered that the field behind the hedge
Grew more distinctly strange as you kept standing
Focused and drawn in by what barred the way.

Wheels within Wheels

I

The first real grip I ever got on things
Was when I learned the art of pedalling
(By hand) a bike turned upside down, and drove
Its back wheel preternaturally fast.
I loved the disappearance of the spokes,
The way the space between the hub and rim
Hummed with transparency. If you threw
A potato into it, the hooped air
Spun mush and drizzle back into your face;
If you touched it with a straw, the straw frittered.
Something about the way those pedal treads
Worked very palpably at first against you
And then began to sweep your hand ahead
Into a new momentum – that all entered me
Like an access of free power, as if belief
Caught up and spun the objects of belief
In an orbit coterminous with longing.

II

But enough was not enough. Who ever saw
The limit in the given anyhow?
In fields beyond our house there was a well
('The well' we called it. It was more a hole
With water in it, with small hawthorn trees
On one side, and a muddy, dungy ooze
On the other, all tramped through by cattle).
I loved that too. I loved the turbid smell,
The sump-life of the place like old chain oil.

And there, next thing, I brought my bicycle.
I stood its saddle and its handlebars
Into the soft bottom, I touched the tyres
To the water's surface, then turned the pedals
Until like a mill-wheel pouring at the treadles
(But here reversed and lashing a mare's tail)
The world-refreshing and immersed back wheel
Spun lace and dirt-suds there before my eyes
And showered me in my own regenerate clays.
For weeks I made a nimbus of old glit.
Then the hub jammed, rims rusted, the chain snapped.

III

Nothing rose to the occasion after that
Until, in a circus ring, drumrolled and spotlit,
Cowgirls wheeled in, each one immaculate
At the still centre of a lariat.
Perpetuum mobile. Sheer pirouette.
Tumblers. Jongleurs. Ring-a-rosies. *Stet*!

Anne Stevenson

About the poet

Anne Stevenson was born in 1933 to American parents living in England. At six months her parents returned to America and she was brought up in New England and Michigan. She went on to study music and languages at Michigan University. She came back to England after marrying a childhood friend, but the marriage broke down and she returned to America in the early 1960s with her four-year-old daughter.

She returned to England after she married again, but she didn't find life as the wife of a Cambridge academic easy. She moved to Scotland and, after her second marriage collapsed, to Hay-on-Wye, where she was a founder of The Poetry Bookshop. In 1981–2 she became Northern Arts Literary Fellow and was appointed as writer in residence at Edinburgh University in 1987.

The subjects covered in her poems reflect her close and clear observation of people and nature. She adopts a wide range of voices in her poems and is similarly at ease with a number of different verse forms. Talking of what she herself admires in poetry she has singled out 'what is controlled, finely wrought yet passionate'.

Her publications include: *Correspondences* (1974), *Travelling Behind Glass* (1974), *Enough of Green* (1977), *Minute by Glass Minute* (1982), *The Fiction Makers* (1985), *The Other House* (1990) and *Four and a Half Dancing Men* (1993).

In the Nursery

I lift the seven months baby from his crib,
a clump of roots.
Sleep drops off him like soil
in clods that smell sunbaked and rich with urine.
He opens his eyes,
two light blue corollas.
His cheek against mine
is the first soft day in the garden.
His mouth makes a bud, then a petal,
then a leaf.
In less than seven seconds
he's blossoming in a bowl of arms.

The Victory

I thought you were my victory
though you cut me like a knife
when I brought you out of my body
into your life.

Tiny antagonist, gory,
blue as a bruise. The stains
of your cloud of glory
bled from my veins.

How can you dare, blind thing,
blank insect eyes?
You barb the air. You sting
with bladed cries.

Snail! Scary knot of desires!
Hungry snarl! Small son.
Why do I have to love you?
How have you won?

Hands

Made up in death as never in life,
mother's face was a mask
set in museum satin.

But her hands. In her hands,
resting not crossing on her paisley dress
(deep combs of her pores,

her windfall palms, familiar routes
on maps not entirely hers
in those stifling flowers), lay

a great many shards of lost hours
with her growing children. As when,
tossing my bike

on the greypainted backyard stairs,
I pitched myself up, through the screen door
arguing with my sister, 'Me? Marry?

Never! Unless I can marry a genius.'
I was in love with Mr Wullover,
a pianist.

Mother's hands moved *staccato* on a fat ham
she was pricking with cloves.
'You'll be lucky, I'd say, to marry a kind man.'

I was aghast.
If you couldn't *be* a genius, at least
you could marry one. How else would you last?

My sister was conspiring to marry her violin teacher.
Why shouldn't I marry a piano
in Mr Wullover?

As it turned out, Mr Wullover died
ten years before my mother.
Suicide on the eve of his wedding, O, to another.

No one said much about why at home. At school
Jenny told me in her Frankenstein whisper,
'He was gay!'

Gay? And wasn't it a good loving thing
to be gay? As good as to be kind
I thought then,

and said as much to my silent mother
as she wrung out a cloth until her knuckles shone,
white bone under raw thin skin.

The Marriage

They will fit, she thinks,
but only if her backbone
cuts exactly into his rib cage,
and only if his knees
dock exactly under her knees
and all four
agree on a common angle.

All would be well
if only
they could face each other.

Even as it is
there are compensations
for having to meet
nose to neck
chest to scapula
groin to rump
when they sleep.

They look, at least,
as if they were going
in the same direction.

from *Correspondences*

A daughter's difficulties as a wife:
Mrs Reuben Chandler to her mother in
New Orleans

SEPTEMBER 3, 1840   CINCINNATI, OHIO

Now that I've been married for almost four weeks,
   Mama,
     I'd better drop you and Papa dear a line.
       I guess I'm fine.

Rube's promised to take me to the Lexington
   buggy races Tuesday, if the weather cools.
     So far we've not been out much.

Just stayed here stifling in hot Cincinnati.
   Clothes almost melt me, Mama, so I've not got out
     my lovely red velvet-and-silk pelisse yet,

or that sweet little lambskin coat with the fur hood.
   The sheets look elegant!
     I adore the pink monogram on the turnover

with exactly the same pattern on the pillowcases!
   Darlings!
     How I wish you could breeze in and admire them!

And the table linen,
   and the bone china,
     and the grand silver candlesticks,

and especially those
   long-stemmed Venetian wine glasses
      with the silver rims.

My, didn't your little daughter
   play the queen the other day
      serving dinner to a whole bevy of bachelors!

To tell the truth, Mama,
   Reuben was a silly to ask them,
      just imagine me, tiny wee me,

hostess to fourteen dragons
   and famished monsters,
      doing battle with fuming pipes and flying plugs.

Poor Rube!
   He doesn't chew and hardly ever smokes.
   He must have felt out of place.

I was frantic, naturally,
   for fear of wine stains and
      tobacco juice on the table cloth,

so I set Agatha to dart in and dab with a towel,
   and told Sue in the kitchen, to brew up some coffee
      quick, before they began speechmaking.

But it was no use.
   They would put me up on a chair after the ices,
      and one of them – Big Tom they call him –

(runs a sizable drygoods business here)
  well, this Tom pulled off my shoe,
    tried to drink wine out of it while

I was dying of laughter,
  and Tom was laughing too, when suddenly
    I slipped, and fell on the Flemish decanter!

It broke.
  Such a terrible pity.
    And so funny at the same time.

I must admit the boys were bricks,
  carrying the tablecloth out to the kitchen,
    holding it out while I

poured hot water from a height,
  just as you always said to.
    Everything would have been all right.

The party could have gone on.
  Then Reuben had to nose in and spoil things,
    sending me to bed!

So the boys went off, kind of sheepish.

Later Reuben said I had disgraced us
  and where was I brought up anyway,
    to behave like a barmaid!

But it wasn't my fault, Mama,
  They were his friends. He invited them.
    I like to give men a good time!

I'm writing this in bed because
   my head thumps and drums every time I move
      and I'm so dog tired!

The only time I sleep is in the morning
   when Reuben has left for the office.
      Which brings up a *delicate* subject, Mama.

I've been thinking and thinking
   wondering whether I'll *ever* succeed in being
      the tender, devoted little wife you wanted me to be.

Because . . . oh, Mama,
   why didn't you tell me or warn me before I was
   married
      that a wife is expected to do it *every night*!

But how could we have guessed?
   Ruby came courting so cool and fine and polite,
      while beneath that gentlemanly, educated
      exterior . . .

well! I don't like to worry you, Mama.
   You know what men are like!
      I remember you said once the dears couldn't
      help it.

I try to be brave.
   But if you *did* have a chance to speak to Papa,
      mightn't you ask him to slip a word,

sort of man to man to Reuben . . .
   about how delicate I am
      and how sick I am every month,

not one of those cows
   who can be used and used?
      Someone's at the door.

I forgot,
   I asked Fanny Daniels to come up this morning
      to help fix a trim for my hat.

I'll have to hustle!
   Give all my love to dear Spooky and Cookie.
      How I miss them, the doggy darlings!

Oceans of hugs and kisses for you, too,
   and for precious Papa,

     From your suffering and loving daughter,

           Marianne

Fragments: Mrs Reuben Chandler writes to her husband during a cholera epidemic

Note: *Most of this journal, written on shipboard, seems to have been destroyed, probably by fire. What remains suggests that Mrs Chandler journeyed to New Orleans without her husband's permission, thus becoming indirectly the cause of her baby's death.*

> EN ROUTE FROM NEW YORK
> TO NEW ORLEANS ABOARD
> THE 'GENERAL WAYNE'

AUGUST, 1849

Two weeks aboard the 'General Wayne'
is little more than a floating hospital
    vomiting spells. I attribute them to
      is truly ill. For two days he has
        in his bunk.
          Belle seems to recover. At least
            fretful which indicates improvement.
          struck by a nervous disorder.
I sleep very little and take no solid food.

                                   (page torn)

(Second page)

Yesterday evening poor little Cookie died.
She was seized suddenly with spasms, poor thing,
and died in an hour. You will accuse me of
          but it was truly frightful.
         I have not slept for weeping.
           only a dog!

                                     (page torn)

(*Third page*)

arrived safely in New Orleans but
 embark. We are all in quarantine
  might be better, but Belle is
   all day by her bedside. Doctor
   plague and gives me no hope
    pray for survival.

(*page torn*)

(*Fourth page*)

have not been able to put pen to
  all over. Our dear little girl
  among the blessed, my beautiful
   authorities let no one near.
   darkies. I am full of
one who was without fault and so
   lies shrouded in my sister's
   blame God and myself, dear
why you have left me without support?

(*page torn*)

A blunder rectified: A final word from Cincinnati businessman, Reuben Chandler, to his runaway wife

APRIL 4, 1855   CINCINNATI, OHIO

Nor do I wish to prolong this tired debate.
I will be brief therefore.
I arrived back from New York late
to find your letter.
So be it.
It was never in the book of my mind
to hold you by force
if I could not restrain you
by the bonds of wifely affection.
Consider yourself free.
On one condition.
That you send both boys to me
entrusting, by law,
their future to my direction.

Of the causes of strife between us -
your selfishness, your vanity, your whims, wife,
your insistent and querulous disobedience,
no more.
It is enough for you to live with your naked conscience
upon which must lie the death of our infant daughter
as her innocent body lies, unfulfilled, in its grave.
Farewell.
Find peace if you can with your sister,
her friends and fashions.
Frivolity is an armor of lace
against the mind's inner vengeance and poisons.

I shall send the boys abroad for their education
as soon as I am advised of a suitable school.
Respect my will with regard to the bills of divorce.
Direct all correspondence to my lawyer, Mr Duval
(you have his address).
Now amen to this farce.

R.C.

From the Motorway

Everywhere up and down the island
Britain is mending her desert;
marvellous we exclaim as we fly on it,
tying the country in a parcel,
London to Edinburgh, Birmingham to Cardiff,
No time to examine the contents,

thank you, but consider the bliss of
sitting absolutely numbed to your
nulled mind, music when you want it,
while identical miles thunder under you,
the same spot coming and going
seventy, eighty times a minute,

till you're there, wherever there
is, ready to be someone in
Liverpool, Leeds, Manchester,
they're all the same to the road,
which loves itself, which nonetheless
here and there hands you trailing

necklaces of fumes in which to be
one squeezed breather among
rich and ragged, sprinter and staggerer,
a status parade for Major Roadworks
toiling in his red-trimmed triangle,
then a regiment of wounded orange witches

defending a shamelessly naked
(rarely a stitch of work on her)
captive free lane,
while the inchlings inch on
without bite or sup, at most
a hard shoulder to creep on,

while there, on all sides,
lie your unwrapped destinations,
lanes trickling off into childhood
or anonymity, apple-scented villages
asleep in their promise of being
nowhere anyone would like to get to.

Terrorist

One morning I despaired of writing more,
     never any more,
when a swallow swooped in, around and out
     the open door,
then in again and batlike to the window,
     against which
beating himself, a suicide in jail,
     he now and then collapsed into
his midnight iridescent combat suit,
     beautiful white markings on the tail.

Inside his balaclava, all he knew
     was something light and airy he had come from
flattened into something hard and blue.
     Thank God for all those drafts I used to
scoop, shove or shovel him to the transom,
     open just enough to let him through.

Off he flew, writing his easy looped
     imaginary line.
No sign of his adventure left behind
     but my surprise
and his – not fright, though he had
     frightened me, those two
bright high-tech bullets called his eyes.
     What they said was
'Fight and fight and fight. No compromise.'

Black Hole

I have grown small
inside my house of words,
empty and hard;
pebble rattling in a shell.

People around me, people.
Maybe I know them.
All so young
and cloudy, not . . . not real.

I can't help being the hole
I've fallen into.
Wish I could tell you
how I feel.

Heavy as mud, bowels
sucking at my head.
I'm being digested.
Remember those moles,

lawn full of them in April,
piles of earth they threw
out of their tunnels. Me, too.
Me, too. That's how I'll

be remembered. Piles
of words, sure, to show
where I was. But nothing true
about me left, child.

Bloody Bloody

Who I am? You tell me
first who you are,
that's manners. And don't shout.
I can hear perfectly well.

Oh, a psychologist.
So you think I'm mad.

Ah, just unhappy.

You must be stupid if you
think it's mad to be unhappy.
Is that what they teach you
at university these days?

I'm sure you're bloody clever.

Bloody? A useful word.
What would *you* say, jolly?

It's bloody bloody,
I assure you,
having to sit up
for a psychiatrist –
sorry, *behavioural psychologist*,
I know there's a difference –
when I want to
lie down and sleep.

The only sensible thing,
at my age, is to be
as you well know
dead, but since they

can't or won't manage
anything like that here,
I consider my right to sleep
to be bloody sacred.

I can't hear you,
I'm closing my eyes.

Please don't open the curtains.

I said *keep the curtains shut*!
Thank you.
            Hate you?
Of course I hate you,
but I can't, in honesty,
say I blame you.
You have to do your job.

There.
That's my telephone.
How fortunate.
You'll avail yourself
of this opportunity, won't you,
to slip tactfully away.

Hello? Yes,
two pieces of good news.
One,
you've just interrupted a most
unnecessary visit,
a young psychological person
is seeing herself out.
Two,
you'll be relieved
to hear I'm worse, much worse.

■ James Fenton

About the poet

James Fenton was born in Lincoln in 1949. He is a graduate of Magdalen College, Oxford and he lives in a riverside farmhouse near Oxford. Now, middle-aged, large, bald and brilliant, he has been described by Peter Porter as 'the most talented poet of his generation'. In 1994 he was elected Professor of Poetry at Oxford University.

He has long and varied experience as a journalist and reporter, and this is fully reflected in his poetry, which ranges from the personal to the political in subject matter, and draws on his experiences of living and working abroad.

Fenton is known by other poets as the last person to share a public reading with. He performs everyone else off the stage, strutting, ranting, punching the air and declaiming his verse in the most dramatic way imaginable. Most of his poetry is contained in two collections, **The Memory of War and Children in Exile** (1983) and **Out of Danger** (1993).

Fenton has neatly encapsulated the variety of his own verse in the following, which he calls *An Amazing Dialogue*:

> *'But this poem is not like that poem!'*
> *'No, you are right, it's not.'*

The Skip

I took my life and threw it on the skip,
Reckoning the next-door neighbours wouldn't mind
If my life hitched a lift to the council tip
With their dry rot and rubble. What you find

With skips is – the whole community joins in.
Old mattresses appear, doors kind of drift
Along with all that won't fit in the bin
And what the bin-men can't be fished to shift.

I threw away my life, and there it lay
And grew quite sodden. 'What a dreadful shame,'
Clucked some old bag and sucked her teeth: 'The way
The young these days . . . no values . . . me,
   I blame . . .'

But I blamed no one. Quality control
Had loused it up, and that was that. 'Nough said.
I couldn't stick at home. I took a stroll
And passed the skip, and left my life for dead.

Without my life, the beer was just as foul,
The landlord still as filthy as his wife,
The chicken in the basket was an owl,
And no one said: 'Ee, Jim-lad, whur's thee life?'

Well, I got back that night the worse for wear,
But still just capable of single vision;
Looked in the skip; my life – it wasn't there!
Some bugger'd nicked it – *without* my permission.

Okay, so I got angry and began
To shout, and woke the street. Okay. *Okay!*
And I was sick all down the neighbour's van.
And I disgraced myself on the par-*kay.*

And then . . . you know how if you've had a few
You'll wake at dawn, all healthy, like sea breezes,
Raring to go, and thinking: 'Clever you!
You've got away with it.' And then, oh Jesus,

It hits you. Well, that morning, just at six
I woke, got up and looked down at the skip.
There lay my life, still sodden, on the bricks;
There lay my poor old life, arse over tip.

Or was it mine? Still dressed, I went downstairs
And took a long cool look. The truth was dawning.
Someone had just exchanged my life for theirs.
Poor fool, I thought – I should have left a warning.

Some bastard saw my life and thought it nicer
Than what he had. Yet what he'd had seemed fine.
He'd never caught his fingers in the slicer
The way I'd managed in that life of mine.

His life lay glistening in the rain, neglected,
Yet still a decent, an authentic life.
Some people I can think of, I reflected
Would take that thing as soon as you'd say Knife.

It seemed a shame to miss a chance like that.
I brought the life in, dried it by the stove.
It looked so fetching, stretched out on the mat.
I tried it on. It fitted, like a glove.

And now, when some local bat drops off the twig
And new folk take the house, and pull up floors
And knock down walls and hire some kind of big
Container (say, a skip) for their old doors,

I'll watch it like a hawk, and every day
I'll make at least – oh – half a dozen trips.
I've furnished an existence in that way.
You'd not believe the things you find on skips.

Hinterhof

Stay near to me and I'll stay near to you –
As near as you are dear to me will do,
 Near as the rainbow to the rain,
 The west wind to the windowpane,
As fire to the hearth, as dawn to dew.

Stay true to me and I'll stay true to you –
As true as you are new to me will do,
 New as the rainbow in the spray,
 Utterly new in every way,
New in the way that what you say is true.

Stay near to me, stay true to me. I'll stay
As near, as true to you as heart could pray.
 Heart never hoped that one might be
 Half of the things you are to me -
The dawn, the fire, the rainbow and the day.

Nothing

I take a jewel from a junk-shop tray
And wish I had a love to buy it for.
Nothing I choose will make you turn my way.
Nothing I give will make you love me more.

I know that I've embarrassed you too long
And I'm ashamed to linger at your door.
Whatever I embark on will be wrong.
Nothing I do will make you love me more.

I cannot work. I cannot read or write.
How can I frame a letter to implore.
Eloquence is a lie. The truth is trite.
Nothing I say will make you love me more.

So I replace the jewel in the tray
And laughingly pretend I'm far too poor.
Nothing I give, nothing I do or say,
Nothing I am will make you love me more.

Serious

Awake, alert,
Suddenly serious in love,
You're a surprise.
I've known you long enough -
Now I can hardly meet your eyes.

It's not that I'm
Embarrassed or ashamed.
You've changed the rules
The way I'd hoped they'd change
Before I thought: hopes are for fools.

Let me walk with you.
I've got the newspapers to fetch.
I think you know
I think you have the edge
But I feel cheerful even so.

That's why I laughed.
That's why I went and kicked that stone.
I'm serious!
That's why I cartwheeled home.
This should mean something. Yes, it does.

Out of Danger

Heart be kind and sign the release
As the trees their loss approve.
Learn as leaves must learn to fall
Out of danger, out of love.

What belongs to frost and thaw
Sullen winter will not harm.
What belongs to wind and rain
Is out of danger from the storm.

Jealous passion, cruel need
Betray the heart they feed upon.
But what belongs to earth and death
Is out of danger from the sun.

I was cruel, I was wrong –
Hard to say and hard to know.
You do not belong to me.
You are out of danger now –

Out of danger from the wind,
Out of danger from the wave,
Out of danger from the heart
Falling, falling out of love.

For Andrew Wood

What would the dead want from us
Watching from their cave?
Would they have us forever howling?
Would they have us rave
Or disfigure ourselves, or be strangled
Like some ancient emperor's slave?

None of my dead friends were emperors
With such exorbitant tastes
And none of them were so vengeful
As to have all their friends waste
Waste quite away in sorrow
Disfigured and defaced.

I think the dead would want us
To weep for what *they* have lost.
I think that our luck in continuing
Is what would affect them most.
But time would find them generous
And less self-engrossed.

And time would find them generous
As they used to be
And what else would they want from us
But an honoured place in our memory,
A favourite room, a hallowed chair,
Privilege and celebrity?

And so the dead might cease to grieve
And we might make amends
And there might be a pact between
Dead friends and living friends.
What our dead friends would want from us
Would be such living friends.

I Saw a Child

I saw a child with silver hair.
Stick with me and I'll take you there.
   Clutch my hand.
   Don't let go.
The fields are mined and the wind blows cold.
The wind blows through his silver hair.

The Blue Vein River is broad and deep.
The branches creak and the shadows leap.
   Clutch my hand.
   Stick to the path.
The fields are mined and the moon is bright.
I saw a child who will never sleep.

Far from the wisdom of the brain
I saw a child grow old in pain.
   Clutch my hand.
   Stay with me.
The fields are mined by the enemy.
Tell me we may be friends again.

Far from the wisdom of the blood
I saw a child reach from the mud.
   Clutch my hand.
   Clutch my heart.
The fields are mined and the moon is dark.
The Blue Vein River is in full flood.

Far from the wisdom of the heart
I saw a child being torn apart.
   Is this you?
   Is this me?
The fields are mined and the night is long.
Stick with me when the shooting starts.

Tiananmen

Tiananmen
Is broad and clean
And you can't tell
Where the dead have been
And you can't tell
What happened then
And you can't speak
Of Tiananmen.

You must not speak.
You must not think.
You must not dip
Your brush in ink.
You must not say
What happened then,
What happened there
In Tiananmen.

The cruel men
Are old and deaf
Ready to kill
But short of breath
And they will die
Like other men
And they'll lie in state
In Tiananmen.

They lie in state.
They lie in style.
Another lie's
Thrown on the pile,
Thrown on the pile
By the cruel men
To cleanse the blood
From Tiananmen.

Truth is a secret.
Keep it dark.
Keep it dark
In your heart of hearts.
Keep it dark
Till you know when
Truth may return
To Tiananmen

Tiananmen
Is broad and clean
And you can't tell
Where the dead have been
And you can't tell
When they'll come again.
They'll come again
To Tiananmen.

Here Come the Drum Majorettes!

There's a girl with a fist full of fingers.
There's a man with a fist full of fivers.
There's a thrill in a step as it lingers.
There's a chance for a pair of salivas -

For the

Same hat
Same shoes
Same giddy widow on a sunshine cruise
Same deck
Same time
Same disappointment in a gin-and-lime

It's the same chalk on the blackboard!
It's the same cheese on the sideboard!
It's the same cat on the boardwalk!
It's the same broad on the catwalk!

There's a Gleb on a steppe in a dacha.
There's a Glob on a dig on the slack side.
There's a Glubb in the sand (he's a pasha).
There's a glib gammaglob in your backside

Saying

Gleb meet Glubb.
Glubb meet Glob.
God that's glum, that glib Glob dig.

'Dig that bog!'
'Frag that frog.'
'Stap that chap, he snuck that cig.'

It's the same ice on the race-track!
It's the same track through the pack-ice!
It's the same brick in the ice-pack!
It's the same trick with an ice-pick!

There's a thing you can pull with your eyeballs.
There's a tin you can pour for a bullshot.
There's a can you can shoot for a bullseye.
There's a man you can score who's an eyesore.

I'm an
Eyesore.
You're the thing itself.
You've a
Price or
You'd be on the shelf.
I'm a loner
In a lonesome town –
Barcelona –
It can get you down.

It's the same scare with a crowbar!
It's the same crow on the barstool!
It's the same stool for the scarecrow!
It's the same bar!

Ho!

Ha!

Like a spark from the stack of a liner
Like a twig in the hands of a dowser
With the force of the fist of a miner
(With the grace and the speed of a trouser)

In a

Blue moon
In a blue lagoon
She's got blue blue bloomers in a blue monsoon.

Wearing blue boots
And a blue zoot suit
He's a cruising bruiser with a shooter and a cute little
Twin blade
Sin trade
In a
Blue brown
New Town.

It's the same hand on the windpipe!
It's the same sand in the windsock!
It's the same brand on the handbag!
It's the same gland in the handjob!

The room is black.
The knuckles crack.
The blind masseuse walks up your back.
The saxophone
Is on its own
Pouring out the *Côtes du Rhône.*

When you're down to your last pair of piastres.
When you're down on your luck down in Przemyśl,
When your life is a chain of disasters
And your death you believe would be sameish,

When the goat has gone off with the gander
Or the goose with the grebe or the grouper
Then – a drum majorette – you can stand her:
She's a brick – she's a gas – she's a trouper

Saying

Jane meet John.
John meet Jane.
Take those jimjams off again
Jezebel.
Just as well.
Join the jive with Jules and June.
Geoffrey, Jesus, Jason, Jim,
Jenny, Jilly, Golly Gee –
If it's the same for you and him
It's the same for you and me:

It's the same grin on the loanshark!
It's the same goon in the sharkskin!
It's the same shark in the skin-game!
It's the same game
Same same

It's the same old rope for to skip with!
It's the same Old Nick for to sup with
    With a long spoon
    To the wrong tune

And it's hard for a heart to put up with!

Carol Ann Duffy

About the poet

Carol Ann Duffy is one of a group of younger writers who have been seen as leading a new generation of poets, and she has won a number of national awards for her poetry. Her published volumes include: **Standing Female Nude** (1985), **Selling Manhattan** (1987), **The Other Country** (1990) and **Mean Time** (1993). She has also edited an anthology for teenagers called **I Wouldn't Thank You for a Valentine**. She was born in Glasgow in 1955 and brought up in Staffordshire, before going to Liverpool University from which she graduated in Philosophy in 1977. She lives in London.

The range of subjects Duffy tackles in her poems is very wide. In dealing with both domestic and political concerns she often uses the device of dramatic monologue to tackle the issues involved. Because her feel for the pitch and rhythm of the human voice is very acute, she often brings her characters to life and makes clear why and how they live as they do.

What one poet has called her 'glorious juggling' with language has also been responsible for her recent wide acclaim. Ruth Padel, in the *Times Literary Supplement* has described Duffy's poetry thus: 'it always knows where it's going and has serious fun on the way. Duffy's is a cabaret art and her leg-flinging technique (the one-word sentences and buried rhymes, the dizzying control of line) can say practically anything.'

Away and See

Away and see an ocean suck at a boiled sun
and say to someone things I'd blush even to dream.
Slip off your dress in a high room over the harbour.
Write to me soon.

New fruits sing on the flipside of night in a market
of language, light, a tune from the chapel nearby
stopping you dead, the peach in your palm respiring.
Taste it for me.

Away and see the things that words give a name to,
　　the flight
of syllables, wingspan stretching to a noun. Test words
wherever they live; listen and touch, smell, believe.
Spell them with love.

Skedaddle. Somebody chaps at the door at a year's end,
　　hopeful.
Away and see who it is. Let in the new, the vivid,
horror and pity, passion, the stranger holding the
　　future.
Ask him his name.

Nothing's the same as anything else. Away and see
for yourself. Walk. Fly. Take a boat till land reappears,
altered forever, ringing its bells, alive. Go on. G'on.
　　Gon.
Away and see.

Comprehensive

Tutumantu is like hopscotch, Kwani-kwani is like
    hide-and-seek.
When my sister came back to Africa she could only
    speak
English. Sometimes we fought in bed because she
    didn't know
what I was saying. I like Africa better than England.
My mother says You will like it when we get our own
    house.
We talk a lot about the things we used to do
in Africa and then we are happy.

Wayne. Fourteen. Games are for kids. I support
the National Front. Paki-bashing and pulling girls'
knickers down. Dad's got his own mini-cab. We watch
the video. I Spit on Your Grave. Brilliant.
I don't suppose I'll get a job. It's all them
coming over here to work. Arsenal.

Masjid at 6 o'clock. School at 8. There was
a friendly shop selling rice. They ground it at home
to make the evening nan. Families face Mecca.
There was much more room to play than here in
    London.
We played in an old village. It is empty now.
We got a plane to Heathrow. People wrote to us
that everything was easy here.

It's boring. Get engaged. Probably work in Safeways
worst luck. I haven't lost it yet because I want
respect. Marlon Frederic's nice but he's a bit dark.
I like Madness. The lead singer's dead good.
My mum is bad with her nerves. She won't
let me do nothing. Michelle. It's just boring.

Ejaz. They put some sausages on my plate.
As I was going to put one in my mouth
a Moslem boy jumped on me and pulled.
The plate dropped on the floor and broke. He asked
    me in Urdu
if I was a Moslem. I said Yes. You shouldn't be eating
    this.
It's a pig's meat. So we became friends.

My sister went out with one. There was murder.
I'd like to be mates, but they're different from us.
Some of them wear turbans in class. You can't help
taking the piss. I'm going in the Army.
No choice really. When I get married
I might emigrate. A girl who can cook
with long legs. Australia sounds all right.

Some of my family are named after the Moghul
    emperors.
Aurangzeb, Jehangir, Batur, Humayun. I was born
thirteen years ago in Jhelum. This is a hard school.
A man came in with a milk crate. The teacher told us
to drink our milk. I didn't understand what she was
    saying,
so I didn't go to get any milk. I have hope and am
    ambitious.
At first I felt as if I was dreaming, but I wasn't.
Everything I saw was true.

Welltread

Welltread was Head and the Head's face was a fist. Yes,
I've got him. Spelling and Punishment. A big brass bell
dumb on his desk till only he shook it, and children
ran shrieking in the locked yard. Mr Welltread. Sir.

He meant well. They all did then. The loud, inarticulate
     dads,
the mothers who spat on hankies and rubbed you away.
But Welltread looked like a gangster. Welltread stalked
the forms, collecting thruppenny bits in a soft black hat.

We prayed for Aberfan, vaguely reprieved. My socks
     dissolved,
two grey pools at my ankles, at the shock of my name
called out. The memory brings me to my feet
as a foul would. The wrong child for a trite crime.

And all I could say was *No.* Welltread straightened my
     hand
as though he could read the future there, then hurt
     himself
more than he hurt me. There was no cause for
     complaint.
There was the burn of a cane in my palm, still
     smouldering.

The Good Teachers

You run round the back to be in it again.
No bigger than your thumbs, those virtuous women
size you up from the front row. Soon now,
Miss Ross will take you for double History.
You breathe on the glass, make a ghost of her, say
South Sea Bubble Defenestration of Prague.

You love Miss Pirie. So much, you are top
of her class. So much, you need two of you
to stare out from the year, serious, passionate.
The River's Tale by Rudyard Kipling by heart.
Her kind intelligent green eye. Her cruel blue one.
You are making a poem up for her in your head.

But not Miss Sheridan. Comment vous appelez.
But not Miss Appleby. Equal to the square
of the other two sides. Never Miss Webb.
Dar es Salaam. Kilimanjaro. Look. The good teachers
swish down the corridor in long, brown skirts,
snobbish and proud and clean and qualified.

And they've got your number. You roll the waistband
of your skirt over and over, all leg, all
dumb insolence, smoke-rings. You won't pass.
You could do better. But there's the wall you climb
into dancing, lovebites, marriage, the Cheltenham
and Gloucester, today. The day you'll be sorry one day.

In Mrs Tilscher's Class

You could travel up the Blue Nile
with your finger, tracing the route
while Mrs Tilscher chanted the scenery.
Tana. Ethiopia. Khartoum. Aswân.
That for an hour, then a skittle of milk
and the chalky Pyramids rubbed into dust.
A window opened with a long pole.
The laugh of a bell swung by a running child.

This was better than home. Enthralling books.
The classroom glowed like a sweet shop.
Sugar paper. Coloured shapes. Brady and Hindley
faded, like the faint, uneasy smudge of a mistake.
Mrs Tilscher loved you. Some mornings, you found
she'd left a good gold star by your name.
The scent of a pencil slowly, carefully, shaved.
A xylophone's nonsense heard from another form.

Over the Easter term, the inky tadpoles changed
from commas into exclamation marks. Three frogs
hopped in the playground, freed by a dunce,
followed by a line of kids, jumping and croaking
away from the lunch queue. A rough boy
told you how you were born. You kicked him, but stared
at your parents, appalled, when you got back home.

That feverish July, the air tasted of electricity.
A tangible alarm made you always untidy, hot,
fractious under the heavy, sexy sky. You asked her
how you were born and Mrs Tilscher smiled,
then turned away. Reports were handed out.
You ran through the gates, impatient to be grown,
as the sky split open into a thunderstorm.

Human Interest

Fifteen years minimum, banged up inside
for what took thirty seconds to complete.
She turned away. I stabbed. I felt this heat
burn through my skull until reason had died.

I'd slogged my guts out for her, but she lied
when I knew different. She used to meet
some prick after work. She stank of deceit.

I loved her. When I accused her, she cried
and denied it. Straight up, she tore me apart.
On the Monday, I found the other bloke
had bought her a chain with a silver heart.

When I think about her now, I near choke
with grief. My baby. She wasn't a tart
or nothing. I wouldn't harm a fly, no joke.

Saying Something

Things assume your shape; discarded clothes, a damp
    shroud
in the bathroom, vacant hands. This is not fiction. This
    is
the plain and warm material of love. My heart assumes
    it.

We wake. Our private language starts the day. We make
familiar movements through the house. The dreams we
    have
no phrases for slip through our fingers into smoke.

I dreamed I was not with you. Wandering in a city
where you did not live, I stared at strangers, searching
for a word to make them you. I woke beside you.

Sweetheart, I say. Pedestrian daylight terms scratch
darker surfaces. Your absence leaves me with the ghost
of love; half-warm coffee cups or sheets, the gentlest
    kiss.

Walking home, I see you turning on the lights. I come
    in
from outside calling your name, saying something.

Valentine

Not a red rose or a satin heart.

I give you an onion.
It is a moon wrapped in brown paper.
It promises light
like the careful undressing of love.

Here.
It will blind you with tears
like a lover.
It will make your reflection
a wobbling photo of grief.

I am trying to be truthful.

Not a cute card or a kissogram.

I give you an onion.
Its fierce kiss will stay on your lips,
possessive and faithful
as we are,
for as long as we are.

Take it.
Its platinum loops shrink to a wedding-ring,
if you like.
Lethal.
Its scent will cling to your fingers,
cling to your knife.

Mrs Skinner, North Street

Milk bottles. Light through net. No post. Cat,
come here by the window, settle down. Morning
in this street awakes unwashed; a stale wind
breathing litter, last night's godlessness. This place
is hellbound in a handcart, Cat, you mark
her words. Strumpet. Slut. A different man
for every child; a byword for disgrace.

Her dentures grin at her, gargling water
on the mantelpiece. The days are gone
for smiling, wearing them to chatter down the road.
Good morning. Morning. Lovely day. Over the years
she's suffered loss, bereavement, loneliness.
A terrace of strangers. An old ghost
mouthing curses behind a cloudy, nylon veil.

Scrounger. Workshy. Cat, where is the world
she married, was carried into up a scrubbed stone step?
The young louts roam the neighbourhood.
Breaking of glass. Chants. Sour abuse of aerosols.
That social worker called her *xenophobic*. When he left
she looked the word up. Fear, morbid dislike, of
    strangers.
Outside, the rain pours down relentlessly.

People scurry for shelter. How many hours
has she sat here, Cat, filled with bitterness
and knowing they'll none of them come?
Not till the day the smell is noticed.
Not till the day you're starving, Cat, and begin
to lick at the corpse. She twitches the curtain
as the Asian man next door runs through the rain.

War Photographer

In his darkroom he is finally alone
with spools of suffering set out in ordered rows.
The only light is red and softly glows,
as though this were a church and he
a priest preparing to intone a Mass.
Belfast. Beirut. Phnom Penh. All flesh is grass.

He has a job to do. Solutions slop in trays
beneath his hands which did not tremble then
though seem to now. Rural England. Home again
to ordinary pain which simple weather can dispel,
to fields which don't explode beneath the feet
of running children in a nightmare heat.

Something is happening. A stranger's features
faintly start to twist before his eyes,
a half-formed ghost. He remembers the cries
of this man's wife, how he sought approval
without words to do what someone must
and how the blood stained into foreign dust.

A hundred agonies in black-and-white
from which his editor will pick out five or six
for Sunday's supplement. The reader's eyeballs prick
with tears between the bath and pre-lunch beers.
From the aeroplane he stares impassively at where
he earns his living and they do not care.

Deportation

They have not been kind here. Now I must leave,
the words I've learned for supplication,
gratitude, will go unused. Love is a look
in the eyes in any language, but not here,
not this year. They have not been welcoming.

I used to think the world was where we lived
in space, one country shining in big dark.
I saw a photograph when I was small.

Now I am *Alien*. Where I come from there are few jobs,
the young are sullen and do not dream. My lover
bears our child and I was to work here, find
a home. In twenty years we would say This is you
when you were a baby, when the plum tree was a
    shoot . . .

We will tire each other out, making our homes
in one another's arms. We are not strong enough.

They are polite, recite official jargon endlessly.
Form F. Room 12. Box 6. I have felt less small
below mountains disappearing into cloud
than entering the Building of Exile. Hearse taxis
crawl the drizzling streets towards the terminal.

I am no one special. An ocean parts me from my love.

Go back. She will embrace me, ask what it was like.
Return. One thing – there was a space to write
the colour of her eyes. They have an apple here,
a bitter-sweet, which matches them exactly. Dearest,
without you I am nowhere. It was cold.

Yes, Officer

It was about the time of day you mention, yes.
I remember noticing the quality of light
beyond the bridge. I lit a cigarette.

I saw some birds. I knew the words for them
and their collective noun. A skein of geese. This cell
is further away from anywhere I've ever been. Perhaps.

I was in love. *For God's sake, don't.*
Fear is the first taste of blood in a dry mouth.
I have no alibi. Yes, I used to have a beard.

No, no. I wouldn't use that phrase. The more you ask
the less I have to say. There was a woman crying
on the towpath, dressed in grey. *Please.* Sir.

Without my own language, I am a blind man
in the wrong house. Here come the fists, the boots.
I curl in a corner, uttering empty vowels until

they have their truth. That is my full name.
With my good arm I sign a forgery. Yes, Officer,
I did. I did and these, your words, admit it.

Glossary: reading the poems

4 *Sambo*   insulting nickname for black people.

6 *sassiness*   mixture of exuberance and impertinence, probably linked to sauciness.

10 *dichty*   wealthy, classy.

  condos   in the USA a condominium (condo) is a block of flats in which each flat is owned by the person who lives there.

14 *fatback*   fatty sort of pork.

15 *septum*   piece of skin dividing the nostrils.

16 *Prescience*   knowledge of events before they take place.

  keloid   disease of the skin.

19 *balks*   gets in the way of.

  prinked   polished.

20 *I Remember, I Remember*   a quotation of the first line of a rather sentimental poem by Thomas Hood (1799-1845) about his childhood home. Larkin's use of it in this very unsentimental poem is ironic.

  Blinding theologies of flowers and fruits   overwhelming mystical feelings about Nature.

  an old hat   an elderly dignified person.

21 *blunt ten-point*   worn-out metal type used for printing; *ten-point* is a size of type.

24 *Annus Mirabilis*   Latin for 'wonderful year'. The poet John Dryden (1631–1700) also wrote a poem with this title about the year 1666, the year of the Great Fire of London.

  Chatterley ban   the novel *Lady Chatterley's Lover* by D.H. Lawrence was written in the late 1920s, but not published in England until 1960. Penguin Books, the publishers, were prosecuted under the

Obscene Publications Act. Penguin Books won the case, and so the 'Chatterley ban' came to an end.

27 *Kennedy*   an imaginary American university.

this old fart   i.e. Larkin himself!

Myra's folks   presumably Jake's wife's relations.

tenure   a permanent job at a university, which Jake would only get by completing his work on Larkin.

put this bastard on the skids   complete my work on Larkin as soon as possible.

Freshman Psych   a first-year university course in Psychology.

28 *losels*   small-time criminals.

loblolly-men   country bumpkins.

the stuff/That dreams are made on   a quotation from Shakespeare's play *The Tempest* (IV.i). In the original, *stuff* means 'material' or 'substance', but Larkin uses it as a pun on *Stuff your pension*.

29 *hunkers*   haunches or hips.

one bodies the other/One's   i.e. the 'toad' work and the 'toad' that inhabits Larkin himself.

30 *jabbering set*   noisy radio.

four aways   predicting four away wins on a football pool.

32 'An Arundel Tomb' is about the medieval tomb of one of the earls of Arundel and his countess in Chichester Cathedral, Sussex.

proper habits   clothes.

pre-baroque   the Baroque period in art, roughly from the mid-sixteenth to the late eighteenth century, valued rich and extravagant decoration. The *pre-baroque* was the period before this, when a plainer style was valued.

lie   Larkin is playing with two meanings of the word: the earl and countess are 'lying' in that their statues are resting horizontally, but are they also 'lying' in holding hands, suggesting to the world that theirs was a perfect love?

tenantry   people who are tenant farmers of the earl's estate (who would have lessened in number over the years).

eyes begin/To look, not read   i.e. because they are unable to understand the Latin inscription.

33 **unarmorial**   not concerned with heraldry and coats of arms.

36 **arcane litany**   literally means an obscure or little-known prayer consisting of a dialogue between priest and congregation. Here the narrator is referring to the way she gets by – asks to be included – in conversation by using well-worn phrases that everyone uses without saying anything original herself.

Masonic   refers to the Freemasons, a society whose members use secret signs and passwords to recognise each other. The narrator suggests her ability to write poetry is a development of her ability to use cliché for her needs as described in the previous stanza. She still relies on secretly observing the system of language and daily rituals as they are used to make contact between people.

not knowing/How right they are   the poet uses a cliché 'how right you are' but adds to its meaning, suggesting that people who are just able to get on with their lives are not aware of quite how many rituals they have mastered to fit in with society and how appropriately they follow the expected patterns of behaviour in growing up.

37 **Born on Monday . . . Buried on Sunday**   the lines in brackets are taken from the traditional nursery rhyme which begins 'Solomon Grundy'; it is then made up of these lines and finishes 'That is the end of Solomon Grundy.'

Novice-naked   *novice* can be used simply to mean inexperienced or to refer to a person who has recently entered a monastery or convent and is not yet a full monk or nun. Both senses of the word would be implied here: the baby is inexperienced and has also only just entered the institution of life.

41 **usher**   used here in its historical sense of under-teacher or teacher's assistant.

42 *indicative*   the *indicative* form of a verb is a form usually used for making statements as exemplified by those included in the reports.

43 **The right degree of immaturity**   the phrase sometimes used when indicating to job applicants that young people need not apply is 'the right degree of maturity'. Here the phrase is changed to imply that the candidate is too old.

45 **He bestrides the wall-to-wall carpeting/Like a colossus**   the poet is playfully comparing this dictator to Cassius's description of Julius Caesar in Shakespeare's play: 'Why man he doth bestride the narrow world/Like a Colossus' (I.ii). The irony is increased because Cassius's description is in fact critical; it is he who masterminds the plot to murder Caesar.

    Laurelled   a garland of laurel leaves was worn as a sign of victory by Roman emperors.

48 **South Sea dancers**   dancers from the Polynesian Islands in the Pacific who would wear garlands round their necks.

    Caulked   fill in the seams of a ship so it won't leak.

    battened   fasten down the tarpaulin fixed over the hatchways of a ship with narrow strips of wood called battens. Both these procedures would prepare a ship for sailing.

49 **autocratic (knee)**   completely in control; in this sense, not at all as wobbly as she feels.

    Like a Degas dancer's   Edgar Degas (1834–1917) was a French Impressionist painter. He is famous for his many paintings of female ballet dancers whose bodies were fit and beautiful.

52 **dipper**   small brown and white bird which dives into water very neatly.

57 **Fourth/Of July to All Fools' Day**   Plath wrote this poem in early 1960, when she was pregnant with her first child, Frieda. Frieda was born on 1 April (All Fools' Day) and therefore must have been conceived on or close to the Fourth of July.

    Atlas   a figure from Greek mythology who was condemned to carry the heavens on his back, which was therefore bent.

Mexican bean   a jumping bean which contains a moth caterpillar.
The caterpillar's movements make the bean jump.

59 *Ebon*   black, like ebony wood.

62 In her time in Devon, Plath kept a hive of bees. 'The Bee Meeting'
records the first time she attended the local beekeepers' society
meeting. It forms an interesting contrast to her prose account of the
same event, ***Charlie Pollard and the Beekeepers*** published in ***Johnny
Panic and the Bible of Dreams*** (1977). This is the first of a series of
five poems concerned with bees written in a week in October
1962. Three of the others are included in this anthology. A basic
knowledge of bees and beekeeping gained from an encyclopaedia
will help to explain many of the detailed points in these poems.

milkweed   a name for plants with milky sap.

64 ***Smoke rolls and scarves***   smoke is puffed into a beehive to quieten
the bees before they are handled. The bees eat their honey,
thinking the hive is on fire, and this calms them.

67 *winged, unmiraculous women*   the worker bees, which are all female.

68 ***A third person***   there is circumstantial evidence to link this 'great
scapegoat' with Ted Hughes, who was stung when wearing a
handkerchief over his head instead of the full beekeeper's mask.

69 *midwife's extractor*   an *extractor* is a device for extracting honey
from honeycombs by centrifugal force. Plath had, in fact,
borrowed one from a local midwife.

70 ***Tate and Lyle***   manufacturer of sugar, which is fed to bees in the
winter as a substitute for the honey which has been taken from
them.

Meissen   German porcelain noted for its pure whiteness.

They have got rid of the men   in the autumn, most of the male
drones are forcibly removed from the hive by the female workers.
Plath, too, was looking ahead to a winter without male company.

72 'A Constable Calls' is the second part of ***Singing School***, a sequence
of six poems in which Heaney explores his own growth as a poet
against the background of Ulster history and politics. This poem tells

of the rather sinister and intimidating visit of a policeman, the agent of the Protestant-controlled government of Ireland, to the Catholic Heaney family.

bevel   groove.

making tillage returns   giving information about what he was growing on his farm.

73 **domesday book**   the record of the survey of the lands of England ordered by William the Conqueror after the Norman invasion of 1066. Heaney implies that Ulster too is a conquered land living under the rule of a foreign power.

flax-dam   pond formed to help the cultivation of flax, a plant grown as the raw material for linen and linseed.

75 **Bluebeard**   a legendary murderer. His hands would have been sticky with blood.

byre   cowshed

77 'The Grauballe Man', and 'Punishment', the poem that follows it in this volume, was one of a number of poems Seamus Heaney wrote about the bodies of Iron Age people discovered in peat bogs in Denmark. The bodies were about two thousand years old, but had been preserved remarkably by the bog water. The skin, hair and clothes were intact, although they had been dyed a deep brown. Most of the bodies seem to have been the victims of ritual murder, or human sacrifice. The Grauballe man has a 'slashed throat' and the girl in 'Punishment' has been drowned.

78 **Dying Gaul**   statue in the Capitoline Museum, Rome, of a Celtic warrior lying wounded on the ground.

hooded victim   victims of sectarian killings in Northern Ireland were sometimes hooded. Heaney is making a link between this man's violent death and the violence of twentieth-century Ulster.

80 **I who have stood dumb** . . .   Heaney is here making a parallel between the fate of this Iron Age woman, drowned for adultery, and the fate of some Catholic women in Ulster in the 1970s who were covered in tar and chained to railings for going out with Protestants or British soldiers.

81 'Act of Union' draws a parallel between the relationship of a husband and a wife to the relationship between England and Ireland. The wife is pregnant, and Heaney compares the unborn baby, just starting to stir, with the colonising Protestant people of Ulster. The title refers both to the political Act of Union in 1800, which made England and Ireland into a single country, and the act of union between a husband and wife which results in the conception of a baby.

82 *flashes* patches of lighter coloured feathers on the wings of birds.

83 *Inishbofin* island off the coast of Galway, in western Ireland.

86 *nimbus* cloud.

> *glit* apparently a word invented by Heaney. What do you think it means?

> *lariat* lasso. The cowgirls stand in the centres of the circles formed by the spinning ropes.

> ***Perpetuum mobile*** Latin for 'perpetual motion'.

> *Jongleurs* French for jugglers, tumblers or minstrels.

> *Stet* Latin for 'let it stand'.

90 *Frankenstein* exaggeratedly dramatic, as in a horror film.

> *gay* originally meaning joyful and light-hearted this word is now also used to describe a man who is homosexual. The mother is clearly aware of the two levels of meaning while the daughter was not at the time.

92 ***Correspondences*** is a book of poems which Stevenson introduces as 'A Family History in Letters'. It consists of a series of documents which records some of the experiences and reflections of the Chandler family from Vermont in the USA at different stages of their lives. The documents span seven generations of the family and are made up mainly of letters, in poetic form, between different members. These are interspersed with occasional newspaper articles, journal extracts and notes, all concerning the fortunes of the family. The three poems in this volume follow one another in the book and are taken from the second generation of the family.

> *Lexington* town in Kentucky, USA.

pelisse   type of cloak for a woman with armholes or sleeves.

93 ***plugs***   pieces of tobacco. Chewing tobacco was a popular habit at the time.

101 ***Major Roadworks . . . witches***   the poet is jokingly imagining major roadworks as an army officer. The orange traffic cones then become his regiment.

    hard shoulder to creep on   the term used to describe the side of the road reserved for emergency stops is also used to echo 'a shoulder to cry on'.

102 ***balaclava***   this refers to the markings on a swallow's head as well as back to the terrorist.

    transom   here short for transom window: a certain type of window (mullioned) divided by a horizontal bar of wood or stone called a transom.

104 'Bloody Bloody' and 'Black Hole' come from a section of one of Anne Stevenson's collections called ***Visits to the Cemetery of the Long Alive***. The section concentrates on depictions of old age.

    behavioural psychologist   someone who studies how the mind works by watching a person's behaviour and uses the observations to change the behaviour if required.

108 ***par-kay***   i.e. parquet, a kind of flooring made of polished wood blocks.

109 ***bat drops off the twig***   slang for 'old woman dies'.

118 'Tiananmen' was written in response to the massacre of students in Tiananmen Square, Beijing, China in 1989. The students were demonstrating against the cruel and dictatorial government of Deng Xiaoping and other 'old and deaf' leaders. They wanted China to become more liberal and more democratic.

120 In 'Here Come the Drum Majorettes!', where sound and rhythm are more important then meaning, notes are rather superfluous, but here are some anyway!

    Gleb on a steppe in a dacha   Gleb was an eleventh-century prince from Kiev, Ukraine, who was allegedly murdered by his brother and who became a saint in the Russian Orthodox Church. A *steppe* is a dry, grassy Russian plain and a *dacha* is a Russian summer-house.

Glob on a dig   a reference to the Danish archaeologist P.V. Glob, who wrote about the bog people who are the subject of some of Seamus Heaney's poems.

Glubb in the sand . . .   a reference to Sir John Bagot Glubb (1897–1986), a British soldier who served mainly in the Middle East, winning the name 'Glubb Pasha' from the local Bedouin. *Pasha* was a Turkish title given to governors and military commanders.

122 **Côtes du Rhône**   French wine.

123 **piastres**   the currency of the former Republic of South Vietnam and several Middle Eastern and North African countries.

Przemyśl   town in south-east Poland.

Old Nick . . . *a long spoon*   the old saying 'he needs a long spoon who sups with the Devil [Old Nick]' means that you will want all your wits about you if you ally yourself with evil.

126 **the National Front**   small, extreme, right-wing political party which favours compulsory deportation of non-white British people.

I Spit on Your Grave   notoriously violent video film.

nan   type of Indian bread.

Mecca   city in Saudi Arabia which is the holiest city in Islam and where the Prophet Muhammad was born. All Muslims face Mecca when they say their prayer.

127 **Urdu**   one of the languages spoken by people who come from Pakistan (and by some people from India).

pig's meat   eating pork is forbidden to Muslims.

Moghul emperors   leaders of a Muslim dynasty in India from the sixteenth to the nineteenth century.

Jhelum   city in Pakistan.

128 **Aberfan**   in 1966 an avalanche of pit waste in the village of Aberfan in South Wales engulfed a school and killed 144 people, including 116 children.

hurt himself/more than he hurt me this refers to the cliché teachers were said often to use before they administered corporal punishment to a child: 'This will hurt me more than it hurts you.'

129 **South Sea Bubble** a period of wild speculation in the shares of the South Sea Company in 1720, which ended with the share price falling rapidly.

Defenestration of Prague an incident in Bohemia in 1618, when two Roman Catholic governors and their secretary were thrown from a window by Protestants, contributing to the start of the Thirty Years War.

The River's Tale poem by Rudyard Kipling (1865-1936) about the River Thames.

Dar es Salaam formerly capital of Tanzania, in East Africa.

Kilimanjaro mountain on the border of Kenya and Tanzania, the highest in Africa.

Cheltenham/and Gloucester a building society.

130 **Tana** Lake Tana in Ethiopia is the source of the Blue Nile.

Khartoum capital of Sudan, where the Blue and White Niles meet.

Aswan town and dam on the Nile in Egypt.

skittle milk bottle that is shaped like a skittle.

Brady and Hindley Ian Brady and Myra Hindley were two child murderers who were convicted in 1966.

Technical terms

alliteration   repetition of the same sound or letter at the beginning of words close to each other, e.g.

A brilliant breaking of the bank

'Annus Mirabilis', page 24

assonance   repetition of similar vowel sounds in words close to each other, e.g. 'grooves' and 'smoothed' in the last two lines of 'Growing Up', page 36.

ballad   a poem which tells a story, usually written in four-line rhyming stanzas. See 'The Skip', page 107.

blank verse   unrhymed poetry written in iambic pentameters. See 'Wheels within Wheels', page 85.

couplet   a pair of rhymed lines, often with the same metre, e.g.

I saw a child with silver hair.
Stick with me and I'll take you there.

'I Saw a Child', page 116

free verse   poetry with no regular rhyme or metre. See 'Coleridge Jackson', page 2.

half-rhyme   rhyme which only rhymes approximately, not fully, e.g. the opening stanza of 'Reasons for Attendance', page 23, where Larkin rhymes 'authoritative' with 'twenty-five' and 'glass', 'face' and 'happiness'.

iambic pentameter   a line of ten syllables divided into five pairs, each with an unstressed syllable followed by a stressed one (it is traditionally associated with the sonnet), e.g.

for what took thirty seconds to complete

'Human Interest', page 131

image   a picture or sense impression built up by the poet in words, e.g. the plant image used throughout 'In the Nursery', page 88.

metaphor   a comparison of one thing with another without using like or as, e.g.

Her body a bulb in the cold

'Wintering', page 70

metre   the pattern of stressed and unstressed syllables in poetry.

onomatopoeia   the use of words which sound like their meaning, e.g. 'slap and plop' in 'Death of a Naturalist', page 74.

personification   giving an object or idea human shape or qualities, e.g. the mirror in 'Mirror', page 61.

quatrain   a verse with four lines.

rhyme scheme   the pattern of rhyming sounds at the ends of lines in a poem. This is usually noted alphabetically, beginning with an *a* for the first line.

simile   a comparison of one thing with another introduced by *like* or *as*, e.g.

The classroom glowed like a sweet shop

'In Mrs Tilscher's Class', page 130

sonnet   a poem of fourteen lines which, conventionally, has a regular rhyme scheme and uses iambic pentameters. See 'Human Interest', page 131.

symbol   something used to represent something else because it has qualities that reflect the characteristics of the thing it is representing, e.g. the swallow's actions and the poet's creative writing process in 'Terrorist', page 102.

Study programme

This study programme is divided into three sections:

- In the first you will find that there are ideas for activities based on individual poems or small groups of poems usually by a single poet.
- The second offers ways of working thematically, combining poems from more than one poet at a time.
- The third section gives suggestions for general activities, using the poems in any combination.

Sometimes a closer reading of a poem can be helped by not approaching the poem in its final form to begin with but by becoming involved, literally, in its construction. In Section 1, activities in italics marked with an * suggest ways the teacher can present the poem initially.

Section I

Maya Angelou

☐ *Coleridge Jackson*

In small groups prepare a performance of the poem consisting of narration and mime or acting.

If you had a chance to ask Coleridge Jackson about his work and family what questions would you ask him and what do you think his replies would be? You could role-play this dialogue.

This poem raises issues not just of racism but the use and abuse of power in general. Discuss any aspects of Coleridge Jackson's relationship with his employer that you recognise from your own experience, past reading or watching of television or film.

2 *Artful Pose*

Using references to a number of her poems, write about what you have learnt of Maya Angelou's experiences of 'lovers false/and hate/and hateful wrath' and some of the means by which she has managed to convey them.

3 *Coleridge Jackson,* **When I Think about Myself** *and* **Still I Rise**

These three poems all deal with racism but the attitudes of the central figures to their situations differ. Discuss what these differences are in small groups. Now look at the different form of each poem. Is it well-suited to convey the different attitudes you've discussed?

Write an essay comparing and contrasting the poems' treatment of racism.

4 *Phenomenal Woman*

The speaker of this poem seems very confident and pleased with herself. Discuss how her personality comes across to the reader. Discuss whether the effect would be different if the speaker were male (*Handsome men* 'wonder where my secret lies', and so on).

5 *Phenomenal Woman,* **Weekend Glory** *and* **Woman Work**

Discuss the way rhythm and rhyme are used to contribute to the impact of these poems. Then, in pairs or small groups, prepare a reading of each poem which makes clear how these elements work.

The three poems are all spoken by women. Discuss and make notes on any similarities or differences between the three women's lives and characters as revealed in these three poems.

6 On Aging

Do you recognise the view of ageing that this woman expresses? Do you think you'll feel the same at this stage of your life?

Imagine you have come to stay in the same house in which the narrator of this poem lives. Her daughter, who knows her well, tells you about the sort of person she is and the best way to relate to her. Using evidence from the poem, write down or role-play what the daughter says to you. Go on to discuss what the poem gains by using the elderly woman as its narrator.

7 Momma Welfare Roll

*[Distribute the poem with the lines cut into separate strips.]

Put these lines into the sequence you feel is most effective. Compare your version with a partner and then with Maya Angelou's original, discussing the effect of any differences. What clues did you use to help you? Is the poet's sequence crucial to its impact?

8 The Lie and Prescience

Both these poems examine pain at separation in a relationship. Discuss their differences and similarities and explain your preference if you have one.

Choose one or both of these poems, and one or both of the poems: 'Phenomenal Woman' and 'Weekend Glory'. Discuss in small groups similarities and differences in areas such as the use of the words, images, rhythm, rhyme, sentence length, development of ideas, the voice and tone of the poem. Write a critical piece on Variety in Maya Angelou's Poetry, using ideas from your discussions.

Philip Larkin

1 Next, Please

In a group of four, read the poem aloud, changing readers at each full stop or exclamation mark. You should have read two sentences each. Now each group member should work on their two sentences, trying to put the sense of them into their own words. When you have all finished, read all your sentences in the same order in which they occur in the poem. Then read the whole poem again.

What do you think the black-sailed ship represents?

2 I Remember, I Remember

In this poem, Larkin is comparing his real childhood, which was 'unspent' in Coventry, with a falsely sentimental or romanticised version. Write two accounts of your own first ten years, one true, plain and unsentimental, and another in which you make it sound more exciting and memorable than it was.

Larkin was very skilled at using complicated verse forms and rhyme schemes while making the poem sound natural and con-versational. See if you can work out the rhyme scheme in this poem. As a clue, ignore the verses and consider the poem nine lines at a time. Does this explain the structural meaning for the last line being by itself?

3 Wild Oats, Reasons for Attendance and Annus Mirabilis

These three poems all deal with love and sex. After reading all three poems carefully, role-play an interview with Philip Larkin about his attitude to women. You could take it in turns to be the interviewer and Larkin.

Use the role-play as a starting point for an extended piece of writing which examines these three poems together.

4 *Poetry of Departures* and *Toads*

These two poems both deal with the subject of work. Larkin's poems both consider the possibility of not working in a regular job and reject it. In pairs discuss:
a) the attractions he describes of a life without regular work;
b) the different reasons he gives for carrying on with a regular job in each of the poems.

5 *The View*

This poem expresses a particular view of middle age. How would you describe this view?

Try to imagine yourself at fifty. Write down what you expect to have achieved by then in terms of your personal life and your career.

Imagine that Larkin's poem was written to an 'agony aunt' in a magazine. Write a reply responding to his complaints and trying to cheer him up.

6 *Posterity*

Jake Balokowsky is an imaginary character. We meet him talking with a friend about the biography he is writing about Larkin. Find evidence in the poem for:
a) Jake's opinions about Larkin.
b) Larkin's opinions about Jake.

How do you think Jake and Larkin would have got on if they had ever met? Construct a role-play or a piece of drama around this intriguing possibility.

7 *Home Is So Sad*

Why does Larkin think that home is sad? What connection can you make between this poem and 'Mr Bleaney'?

8 *Mr Bleaney*

Pick out all the details of the room and the view that together make up the picture of Mr Bleaney's environment.

Discuss with a partner the degree to which we make judgements about people on the basis of where they live.

Why do you think the narrator of the poem takes the room? What do you think this shows about how he feels about himself?

9 *An Arundel Tomb*

To get the most from this poem, you will need to study it closely and read it repeatedly. The Glossary will help you with some of it, and there will be other words that you may need to look up in a dictionary. The kind of approach we outline in the section 'How to read a poem' should help you.

When you feel confident with the poem, write a study of it showing how the stages of Larkin's thoughts while looking at the tomb lead him to the poem's conclusion.

U.A. Fanthorpe

1 *Growing Up* and *Growing Out*

[Present the verses of either poem out of their original sequence.]

Reorder the poem in the sequence you feel is most appropriate. Compare your version with a partner's and then with U.A. Fanthorpe's original. Discuss what clues you used to help you sequence the poem.

* [Present the verses of both poems which have been cut up and mixed together.]

Separate the poems and order them into the sequences you feel are most appropriate. Compare your version with a partner's, discussing contrasts in the two poems' content and form.

Write an essay comparing and contrasting the two poems' treatment of the process of growing up.

You might like to try writing your own poem on the same theme.

2 *Half-past Two*

Discuss how the poet has tried to catch the thought processes of a small child.

In small groups prepare a performance of the poem in which you try to highlight the child's situation through the way you organise the reading.

3 *Reports*

* [*Present this poem with the last verse omitted.*]

Read through the poem and try to write your own last verse (three lines).

Make a list of the phrases used in this poem from reports. Having read the poem, discuss in small groups:
a) what you think U.A. Fanthorpe would see as the shortcomings of each particular phrase;
b) how you think reports should be written, if at all.

4 *You Will Be Hearing from Us Shortly*

Do you recognise this situation from your own experience or anything you have read or watched?

Write a commentary alongside the poem which conveys the unspoken thoughts of the interviewer(s) and interviewee. This could be done in the form of a performance with separate people speaking the thoughts that are not voiced aloud. Discuss how the original poem is affected by this addition. Now write about the way in which the form of Fanthorpe's poem contributes to its impact.

5 *Dictator*

* [*Take out the words 'colossus', 'comma', 'semicolon', 'draughts', 'assumed', 'muscles', 'fullstop' and 'liquidated' before you present the poem.*]

What could fill the gaps? Compare your version with a partner's and then with Fanthorpe's completed poem.

Write about how she has built up the central figure and how effective you find her poem. You could draw or find a picture which seems to match the figure she has created in the poem to include with your writing.

6 *Old Man, Old Man*

Can you identify, from your own experience, with any aspects of the narrator's situation here?

Working with a partner write down what you consider to be five true statements and five false statements about this poem. You should include references to the character of the old man, the way he's described and the relationship of the old man and the narrator.

Now share your statements with another pair and see if they agree. Collect all the statements considered to be true made by the class, discuss them and then complete some critical writing on the poem with a title of your own choice.

7 *After Visiting Hours*

Provide a summary of the poem in one sentence of prose for each verse. Discuss and/or write about what has been lost in terms of the language, rhythm, images, tone of voice, etc.

8 *Casehistory: Alison (head injury)*

Using the evidence from the poem, write a doctor's report on Alison's condition. Discuss how the effect on the reader is changed from the original poem.

9 *After Visiting Hours, Casehistory: Alison (head injury)* and **Patients**

Choose two or three of the poems above and discuss Fanthorpe's depiction of patients.

10 *Going Under*

* [*Leave out the title when presenting this poem.*]

Discuss what would be an appropriate title after reading the poem. Share your thoughts on the poet's original title.

Sylvia Plath

1 *Mushrooms*

This poem is an extended example of the poetic technique of personification, in that the poet is imagining what kind of personalities mushrooms would have if they could think and speak.

Discuss with a partner the details of the mushrooms' characteristics. What is the effect of the persistent rhythm which runs through the poem?

You might like to try writing a poem of your own which personifies a plant of some sort.

2 *Metaphors*

This poem is a sort of puzzle, consisting of a series of metaphors for the same thing. Work out what the poem is about with a partner.

When you have a theory, consider the significance of the number of syllables in each line, the number of lines, and even the number of letters in the title.

3 *You're* and *Morning Song*

These two poems are both about babies, 'You're' was written around the sixth month of Plath's first pregnancy and 'Morning Song' when her first child was about ten months old.

'You're' works largely through metaphor and simile. With a partner, list all the images she uses for the unborn child. Try to sum up what range of emotions she has about the baby.

Now go through the same process with 'Morning Song'. What similarities and differences can you find between what the two poems say about the experience of motherhood?

4 *Blackberrying*

It is interesting to compare this poem with Seamus Heaney's poem 'Blackberry-Picking' which is also in this volume. What in Plath's poem suggests that her experience of blackberrying was solitary? How does this contrast to the way Heaney went blackberrying? How do the first two stanzas of Plath's poem contrast with the third in tone and atmosphere? How does Heaney's first stanza contrast with his second?

Which poet's description of the physical sensations, sights, sounds and smells of picking blackberries seems to you the most vivid, immediate and memorable?

5 *Mirror*

* [*Distribute copies of the poem with the title removed.*]

In small groups, read the poem carefully and suggest a title for it.

Read through the second stanza substituting 'man' for 'woman', 'boy' for 'girl' and male pronouns for female ones. Then discuss how far you think this is a poem about a mirror, and how far it is about being a woman.

6 *The Bee Meeting, The Arrival of the Bee Box, Stings* and *Wintering*

These four poems were all written within a week and share a common theme of bees and beekeeping. Although each poem can be studied separately, it is useful and interesting to consider them as a collection. There follows work on each of the poems and then some suggestions for work on them as a group.

The questions on each poem are meant to lead towards a fuller understanding of them all. They can be considered individually, in pairs or in small groups.

● *The Bee Meeting*

If possible, read *Charlie Pollard and the Beekeepers*, which is Sylvia Plath's journal entry covering the events in the poem. It is in a collection of prose pieces by Plath called *Johnny Panic and the Bible of Dreams* (Faber, 1977).

Write a detailed comparison of the two accounts, paying particular attention to any contrasts in the language used and what the writer seems to feel about her experience. What is the effect of there being so many questions in the poem? What do you think Plath has achieved by turning her journal entry into a poem?

● *The Arrival of the Bee Box*

What kind of a first impression of the bee box do we get from the first stanza?

What are the stages of the poet's changing attitude towards the bees in the box?

Explore and explain the 'Roman mob' imagery in the poem.

- **Stings**

Use the Glossary to help you understand some of the references in this poem.

From your researches on the subject of beekeeping, what operation is being carried out by Plath and her companion in the first four stanzas?

What parallels between her own life and the lives of the worker bees does Plath begin to explore in the middle of the poem?

What impression do you get of the poet's attitude towards the 'third person' who is introduced in the eighth stanza?

- **Wintering**

How does the poet use light and colour in this poem?

What parallels does Plath find between her own situation and that of the bees?

- *The four 'bee' poems*

Now that you have studied the four 'bee' poems in depth, write an extended essay on the way Plath's attitude to the bees develops throughout the poems, from fear and hostility to identification and sympathy.

Seamus Heaney

☐ *A Constable Calls*

In pairs, list the ways in which Heaney's choice of language to describe the constable and his equipment make him a menacing figure in this poem.

2 *Death of a Naturalist* and *Blackberry-Picking*

These poems are both divided into two sections. In groups, discuss the difference in the poet's attitude to the frogs and the blackberries in the two sections of each poem, and the way this is made clear in the words he uses.

Now consider the title 'Death of a Naturalist'. Why do you think Seamus Heaney called the poem this, rather than something like 'Frogs'? Do you think it would serve just as well for a title to 'Blackberry-Picking'?

Now write an essay about both poems, trying to make as many connections between them as you can.

3 *Mid-Term Break*

The exact nature of what the poem is about only emerges in the last few words of the poem. In pairs, work out the clues that we are given throughout the poem as to what has happened. Why do you think Heaney has chosen to write the poem in this way?

4 *The Grauballe Man* and *Punishment*

Read the entry in the Glossary for these poems, which will give you some background about their subject. In 'The Grauballe Man', Heaney writes 'I first saw his twisted face/in a photograph'. Try to find more photographs of the subjects of these poems. The best source is a book called **The Bog People** by P.V. Glob (Faber, 1969, and Paladin, 1971), although you may also find photographs in encyclopaedias.

In both poems, Heaney tries to build up a mental picture of the body by the use of similes and metaphors, by saying what the different parts of the bodies look like or remind him of. Explore this way of writing by listing and trying to explore each image.

For example:

> 'poured in tar': the man's body is black like tar, shiny like a liquid, and squashed so that it looks like something set in a mould.
>
> 'pillow of turf': the turf is soft and the man's head is resting on it.

. . . and so on.

5 *Act of Union*

This poem, like Philip Larkin's 'Next, Please', is an example of an extended metaphor, where the poet is exploring in detail the parallels between two subjects that might appear very different. Explore this technique by dividing a piece of paper in three, with the headings *Husband/England, Wife/Ireland* and *Unborn Baby/Ulster*. Under each heading, explore the parallels that Heaney finds between the two subjects in the poem.

6 *Changes*

The poem is addressed to a specific person ('As *you* came with me in silence'). Who do you think this person is, and what do you think is the relationship between this person and the writer?

What do you make of the advice the writer gives in the last two verses? Why has the incident described been worth remembering?

7 *Seeing Things (I)*

The second line uses just five words to conjure up the sights, sounds and smells of the setting. Think of a place you know well, and try to recreate it in five words, as Heaney has done. Then use your line as the second line of a poem describing an incident in your setting.

8 *Field of Vision*

The poem explores how what may at first seem a barrier to communication (a wheelchair, a gate) can serve as a focus for a deeper level of perception. Staying true to what Heaney tells us, and adding details from your own imagination, write an account of a day in the woman's life as written by herself.

9 *Wheels within Wheels*

Write down three words to summarise what you think are the three most important things that the poem is about. When you are ready, discuss and compare your words with a partner's, and agree on a joint list. Now form a group of four and go through the same process.

Anne Stevenson

1 *In the Nursery*

* [*In order to focus on the imagery, present this poem with the following words taken out and listed separately: 'a clump of roots', 'soil', 'clods', 'corollas', 'bud', 'petal', 'leaf', 'blossoming', 'bowl'.*]

Discuss and/or write about the effectiveness of the imagery after sharing your versions and looking at the original.

2 *In the Nursery* and *The Victory*

Using these two poems, compare and contrast the poet's treatment of attitudes towards a baby. Include comments on which one you prefer and why.

3 *Hands*

Looking back at your own childhood, can you remember incidents similar to the one described in the second half of this poem? Discuss the character of the mother and the way it is constructed. Include in your discussion why Stevenson chose to put only one line of the mother's own voice into her poem. Then write a diary entry for the mother reflecting on the episode referred to in the poem.

4 *The Marriage*

* [Rewrite each verse of this poem as prose.]

How would you set out these four sentences as four verses of a poem? Write them out in the way you think most appropriate and then compare your version with a partner's, justifying your reasons for your layout.

Now compare your versions with Stevenson's, discussing any differences. Go back to the prose version you began with and, comparing it with Stevenson's poem, consider what the form of the poem contributes to its impact.

5 *A daughter's difficulties as a wife*

Imagine you are the mother or father reading the letter/poem from your daughter, and thinking aloud about what lies behind her words. Write down your thoughts, and the reason for them. You could then role-play a dialogue between the mother and father discussing the letter.

Using evidence from the poem, write down Reuben's thoughts after the first few weeks of his marriage.

6 *Fragments*

Discuss in pairs and/or small groups what the form of this poem contributes to its impact.

7 *A daughter's difficulties as a wife, Fragments* and *A blunder rectified*

Write character studies of Marianne and Reuben backing up your reflections on their characters with detailed evidence from the poems. Think particularly about the words each character uses and the tone of their voice. You might write these in the form of profiles for a newspaper article.

8 *From the Motorway*

In pairs, role-play an interview with Anne Stevenson in which she is asked about her views on the nation's road building policy. Use as many of the ideas and images in the poem as you can if you are playing the poet. As the interviewer you might like to express your agreement or opposition to her views. Discuss in your pairs, and then write about, how the poetic form helps the expression of her ideas.

9 *Terrorist*

This poem provides a good example of how a symbol can be used in a poem. Discuss and then write about the relationship between the bird and the poet's writing.

Try developing a symbol in writing to illustrate a process in your own life, e.g. writing a GCSE essay; getting up in the morning; quarrelling with someone.

10 *Black Hole* and *Bloody Bloody*

Perform a reading of these two poems.

Compare and contrast these two poems' portrayal of people who are ageing and frustrated.

James Fenton

1 *The Skip*

Like many of Fenton's poems, this one cries out to be read aloud. In groups of about four, read the poem to each other, changing readers at every full stop.

'Loused it up' and 'nicked' are both examples of slangy, informal language rather than Standard English. What other examples can you find from the poem? Why do you think James Fenton has chosen to use this register in the poem?

This poem uses the poetic form known as ballad. Ballads tell stories, and often use four-line stanzas with the second and fourth lines rhyming. In this poem, Fenton rhymes the first and third lines of each verse as well. He also uses a regular ten-syllable line of five stresses, known as the iambic pentameter, which you may be familiar with from studying Shakespeare's plays. Try to write a ballad of your own, deciding which of these rules you will attempt to follow.

2 Hinterhof

Look in detail at the similes in the poem. Think up some similes of your own for nearness, newness and truth.

3 Nothing

In a small group discuss how the last line of each stanza sums the stanza up, and how the last line of the poem sums the whole poem up.

4 Hinterhof, Nothing, Serious and Out of Danger

All of these poems deal with love and relationships. In a pair, match these descriptions of stages of a relationship to the poems:
a) being in love and hoping it will last for ever;
b) realising that your love will never be returned;
c) realising that a relationship is coming to an end;
d) falling in love with an old friend.

Now write a study of these four love poems, paying close attention to the emotions which are being expressed.

5 *For Andrew Wood*

The first two lines ask a question which the rest of the poem attempts to answer. What answers does Fenton provide, firstly about our immediate reactions to the death of a friend, and secondly about our longer-term feelings? Do you agree with him, or have you any alternative answers to the question?

6 *I Saw a Child*

This poem springs out of Fenton's experiences as a war reporter in Vietnam and Cambodia. Discuss how he builds up a sense of danger in the poem. What words and phrases are repeated? Why do you think he wants to emphasise these?

7 *Tiananmen*

Find out as much as you can about the Tiananmen Square massacre in Beijing, China in June 1989. One account, by the BBC reporter John Simpson, is in *Granta* (volume 28: **Birthday Special!**, Penguin, 1989). From your researches, say who 'the dead' and the 'cruel men' are. Have the cruel men been able to keep the truth dark? Have they died and been laid in state yet? Have the dead come again to Tiananmen?

How does Fenton make his own feeling on the massacre clear in the poem?

8 *Here Come the Drum Majorettes!*

This poem has to be read aloud. Try to get a confident reader to give you a performance to start you off. Now it's your turn! In groups of about four, practise for a performance. To make it sound good, concentrated rehearsal is needed. Nearly all the words in it are said as they are spelled, so it's not a disaster if you don't understand them. The Glossary will help if you are curious. Two possible difficulties are:

- *Côtes du Rhône* is pronounced 'coat du roan';

- *Przemyśl* is pronounced 'pshemishl'; Fenton makes it rhyme with 'sameish'.

Now try to work out which sections of the poem share the same rhythms. For a start, the sections starting with these lines all share the same 'diddy dum diddy dum diddy dum dum' rhythm:

> There's a girl with a fist full of fingers . . .
> There's a Gleb on a steppe in a dacha . . .
> There's a thing you can pull with your eyeballs . . .

Decide how you are going to break the poem up among the readers. Are you going to change the reader every line? Have a new reader for each section? Have a reader responsible for all the sections which share the same rhythm?

After a period for rehearsal, perform your version to the other groups.

Discuss which group's version was the most successful, and what ingredients go to make up a good poetry performance.

This poem has been called *surreal*. Surrealism is a form of art or literature that escapes the control of reason and claims to express the unconscious mind. It often relies on putting together objects or ideas that we don't normally associate with one another, for example 'It's the same stool for the scarecrow' or 'With the grace and the speed of a trouser'. You could try writing your own surreal performance poem.

Carol Ann Duffy

Away and See

Look carefully at what the narrator of this poem is urging her listener to 'away and see' and the tone of voice in which she does so. Then imagine yourself as a parent or adult friend of someone about to leave home. Write them a letter or poem, describing what you would urge them to 'away and see'.

2 *Comprehensive*

Think of a small group of people you know who often find themselves together though there may be many differences between them. Write a verse or passage of prose for each in which they either describe a memory from their early childhood or their ambitions for the future. If appropriate, you could write this without mentioning the people's names so they, or other friends, could try to guess who was being described.

3 *Welltread*

Can you remember any teacher from your primary school as vividly as Carol Ann Duffy remembers Welltread? Discuss Welltread's character. How is it constructed by Duffy in the poem? Now imagine you are Welltread and write your account of the incident remembered in the poem.

Prepare a reading of the poem with mime to back it up.

4 *The Good Teachers*

Write one school-day entry in the diary of the girl described, using evidence from the poem to fill in the details of her day.

Choose one of the teachers and write a report in the last year of the girl described.

5 *In Mrs Tilscher's Class*

Which parts of the poem in particular remind you of your own memories of primary school? Look at how Duffy captures details in her poems. Try to write a list of snapshots from your own memories. You could then work these into a poem or prose piece.

6 *Welltread,* **The Good Teachers** *and* **In Mrs Tilscher's Class**

Choose two of the three poems above. Compare and contrast the poet's treatment of childhood memories of school. Think about the nature of the memories themselves and the methods she has used to convey them. Include references to which one you prefer and why. Discuss notes for your essay in small groups or class first.

7 *Human Interest*

This poem is a sonnet like 'Saying Something' which follows it but, unlike that poem, it has a clearly defined rhyme scheme (see 'Technical terms', page 149). Work out what this is and then discuss its contribution to the poem. Think particularly about these two points:

- Is it important which words the poet has chosen to rhyme together? e.g. by linking 'complete' and 'heat' does this reinforce the fact that their meaning is linked: the completion of the murder was accompanied by the burning heat through his skull? And what about 'inside' and 'died' and so on?

- You will have worked out that the first eight lines (called the octave) are linked by their rhyme scheme; why then has the poet chosen to place the last of these lines at the beginning of the next six lines (called the sestet)? Does it gain more emphasis this way? Is there any reason why she might want this to be the case?

The sonnet over the ages has often been associated with an expression of love. How would this traditional association add a further comment on the content of the poem?

You might like to go on to scan the poem's *metre* and explore how interruptions in the *stress pattern* are used to contribute to the impact of the poem, e.g. why do the first and fourth lines not stick to the *iambic pentameter* of the second and third? What might the poet want to stand out by this change to the convention? Does she use this method in the other verses of the poem? Also, the ninth line has one extra beat – the stressed second half of 'apart': is this significant?

When you have finished your analysis write an essay bringing together your thoughts on the poem.

8 *Human Interest*, *Saying Something* and *Valentine*

The narrators in these three poems are each concerned in different ways to convey love for someone. Choose two or three of them and first, in small groups, make notes on:

- what you have learnt of the person talking and the nature of their relationship;
- how this is conveyed and whether the means are effective;
- whether you have any personal preference and if so why.

Now write an essay using either two or three of the poems, comparing and contrasting their portrayal of love.

9 *Mrs Skinner, North Street*

Discuss and make notes on the sort of details Duffy uses to build up the picture of Mrs Skinner. Use the same techniques to write a piece of prose or poetry about someone you know who is isolated in some way from the people among whom he or she lives.

10 *War Photographer*

Imagine you are the war photographer. Using the details in the poem write a description of your job. Before you start, look carefully at whether we are given any clues as to his attitude towards his job and if so include these in the description.

11 *Deportation* and *Yes, Officer*

What similarities and differences can you find in the experiences of the narrators and the way they are depicted in these two poems?

Section 2

In this section you will find some lists of poems which can be discussed and written about together because they are linked by a theme or an idea. These lists are not exhaustive and are intended to get you thinking about how poems can be associated with one another. You will want to add to them from the poems in this anthology, choosing poems or poets that you particularly admire. The lists are followed by some suggestions for how to work with thematic groups of poems.

Babies
Metaphors; You're; Morning Song (Plath)
In the Nursery; The Victory (Stevenson)

School
Half-past Two; Reports (Fanthorpe)
Death of a Naturalist (Heaney)
Comprehensive; Welltread; The Good Teachers;
    In Mrs Tilscher's Class (Duffy)

Parents
Morning Song (Plath)
Hands (Stevenson)

Growing up
Growing Up; Growing Out (Fanthorpe)
Death of a Naturalist; Blackberry-Picking (Heaney)
Away and See (Duffy)

In love
Wild Oats (Larkin)
Hinterhof; Serious (Fenton)
Saying Something; Valentine (Duffy)

Couples in bed
Going Under (Fanthorpe)
Act of Union (Heaney)
The Marriage (Stevenson)

Problematic love relationships
Prescience (Angelou)
Wild Oats; Annus Mirabilis (Larkin)
The Marriage; A daughter's difficulties as a wife (Stevenson)
Nothing (Fenton)
Human Interest (Duffy)

Old age
On Aging (Angelou)
The View (Larkin)
Old Man, Old Man (Fanthorpe)
Black Hole; Bloody Bloody (Stevenson)
Mrs Skinner, North Street (Duffy)

Reflections on death
Next, Please; The View; An Arundel Tomb (Larkin)
Mid-Term Break; The Grauballe Man; Punishment (Heaney)
For Andrew Wood (Fenton)

Being a woman
Phenomenal Woman; Weekend Glory; Woman Work (Angelou)
Mirror; Wintering (Plath)

Repression
Coleridge Jackson; When I Think about Myself; Still I Rise (Angelou)
A Constable Calls (Heaney)
Tiananmen (Fenton)
Yes, Officer (Duffy)

Portraits
Coleridge Jackson; Momma Welfare Roll (Angelou)
Mr Bleaney (Larkin)
Dictator; Old Man, Old Man; Casehistory: Alison (head injury)
   (Fanthorpe)
Field of Vision (Heaney)
Hands (Stevenson)
Comprehensive; Welltread; Mrs Skinner, North Street (Duffy)

1 Create a list of your own based on a single theme. A few ideas might be:

- The world of work
- Loneliness
- Outsiders
- The language of authority
- What we learn from the past
- Living in the country
- Family ties

2 Make an individual, group or class anthology based on a theme. Below each poem should be a short piece of writing which shows how the poem relates to the theme and, perhaps, how it is similar or different to the others in the collection. You might choose to illustrate the anthology and then present it as a book or display.

3 Use the material you have collected for an anthology in a different way. For example, produce a 'magazine' programme for radio or television. This will give you the opportunity to read and perform poems as well as present them visually. You will need to include in your programme a general introduction, a short commentary on each poem and a section on how it might relate to the theme. You might also wish to include some role-played interviews with authors.

4 You could compare and contrast two or three poets' treatment of the same theme. For instance, how do James Fenton, Carol Ann Duffy and Philip Larkin deal with the theme of love in their poetry? What are the experiences and attitudes revealed in their poems, how do they compare, and what forms do they use to convey their ideas? In your view, are they equally successful? A study of this kind would make an excellent literary essay, particularly if you used quotations to prove your findings.

Section 3

This section contains further ideas for exploring and enjoying the poems in this anthology and elsewhere. These ideas can be used with any poet or set of poems you choose.

1 Compare two poets with similar backgrounds. For example, Anne Stevenson and Sylvia Plath are both Americans who spent much of their lives in England. James Fenton and Philip Larkin are both from the English middle class and were educated at Oxford.

2 Contrast two poets with very different profiles: for example the introvert, white, male, English Larkin with the extrovert, black, female American Angelou.

3 You should have learned a lot that would be useful to younger students while working on this anthology. Write a guide for next year's GCSE class, taking account of how far their understanding and enjoyment of poetry is likely to have progressed so far?

4 Produce a class anthology of original poems which are inspired by the style and subject matter of one or more of the poets in the anthology. The class anthology could be published, or read to other classes at an assembly. Include some information on the poets who inspired your poems, and examples of their work.

5 Make a radio programme on tape based on *Desert Island Discs*, in which you present readings of some of your favourite poems from the anthology linked by your comments about them.

6 Run a poetry speaking competition, in which you reward speakers or groups of speakers for the clarity and inventiveness of their readings.

Pearson Education Limited
Edinburgh Gate, Harlow,
Essex, CM20 2JE, England
and Associated Companies throughout the world.

First published 1995
Eighth impression 2004
ISBN 0 582 25401 9

Editorial material set in 10/12 pt Gill Sans Light
Printed in Singapore (MPM)

Consultants: Geoff Barton and Jackie Head

'Next, Please', Mr Bleaney', 'An Arundel Tomb', 'Home is So Sad', 'Wild Oats', 'Annus Mirabilis', 'Posterity' and 'The View' from *Collected Poems* by Philip Larkin, edited by Anthony Thwaite, 'Metaphors', 'Mushrooms', 'You're', 'Morning Song', 'Blackberrying', 'Mirror', 'The Bee Meeting', 'Arrival of the Bee Box', 'Stings' and Wintering from *Collected Poems* by Sylvia Plath, edited by Ted Hughes; The Marvell Press for 'Reasons for Attendance', 'Poetry of Departures', 'I Remember, I Remember' and 'Toads' from *The Less Deceived* by Philip Larkin; Oxford University Press for 'The Victory', 'The Marriage', 'A Daughter's Difficulties as a Wife', 'Fragments' and 'A Blunder Rectified' from *Selected Poems 1956–1986* © Anne Stevenson (1987), 'In the Nursery' and 'From the Motorway' from *The Other House* © Anne Stevenson (1990), 'Bloody Bloody', 'Black Hole' and 'Terrorist' from *Four and a Half Dancing Men* © Anne Stevenson(1993), 'Hands' from *The Fiction Makers* © Anne Stevenson 1985; The author's agent on behalf of James Fenton for 'The Skip' and 'Nothing' from *The Memory of War and Children in Exile* (Penguin Books Ltd 1983), 'Out of Danger', 'Serious', 'Hinterhof', 'I Saw a Child', 'Tiananmen', 'Here Come the Drum Majorettes', 'For Andrew Wood' and 'An Amazing Dialogue' from *Out of Danger* (Penguin Books Ltd 1993); Peterloo Poets for 'Casehistory: Alison (Head Injury)', 'After Visiting Hours', 'Reports', 'You Will Be Hearing From Us Shortly', 'Patients' and 'Growing Up' from *Selected Poems* © U.A. Fanthorpe (Peterloo Poets and King Penguin 1986), 'Growing Out' from *Standing To* © U.A. Fanthorpe (Peterloo Poets 1982), 'Old Man, Old Man' from *A Watching Brief* © U.A. Fanthorpe (Peterloo Poets 1987), 'Dictator', 'Going Under' and 'Half-past Two' from *Neck-Verse* © U.A. Fanthorpe (Peterloo Poets 1992); Virago Press Ltd for 'When I Think about Myself' and 'Artful Prose' from *Just Give Me a Cool Drink of Water 'fore I Piiie* by Maya Angelou, 'Phenomenal Woman', 'Momma Welfare Roll', 'Woman Work', 'Still I Rise', 'The Lie', 'On aging' and 'Prescience' from *And Still I Rise* by Maya Angelou (1986), 'Coleridge Jackson' from *I Shall Not Be Moved* by Maya Angelou (1990), 'Weekend Glory' from *Maya Angelou The Complete Collected Poems* (1994).

We are grateful to the following for permission to use copyright photographs:

Virago Press for Maya Angelou; Faber & Faber Ltd for Philip Larkin; Peterloo Poets for U. A. Fanthorpe; Penguin Books Ltd for Sylvia Plath, Seamus Heaney and James Fenton; the Grauballe Man is from P. V. Glob: *The Bog People* (Paladin, 1971); Oxford University Press for Anne Stevenson; Anvil Press Poetry for Carol Ann Duffy.